Narrative Theory and *Adaptation.*

FILM THEORY IN PRACTICE

Series Editor: Todd McGowan

FILM THEORY IN PRACTICE

Narrative Theory and *Adaptation.*

JASON MITTELL

Bloomsbury Academic India
An imprint of Bloomsbury Publishing Inc

BLOOMSBURY
NEW DELHI • LONDON • OXFORD • NEW YORK • SYDNEY

BLOOMSBURY INDIA
Bloomsbury Publishing India Pvt. Ltd
Second Floor, LSC Building No. 4, DDA Complex, Pocket C–6&7,
Vasant Kunj, New Delhi 110070

BLOOMSBURY, BLOOMSBURY ACADEMIC INDIA and the Diana logo are trademarks of Bloomsbury Publishing Plc

First published 2017
First published in India 2023

This edition published with permission from Bloomsbury Publishing Plc, 50 Bedford Square, London, WC1B3DP, UK

British Library Cataloguing-in-Publication Data
A catalogue record for this book is available from the British Library

Library of Congress Cataloging-in-Publication Data
A catalog record for this book is available from the Library of Congress

ISBN: 978-93-93715-86-9

Typeset by Deanta Global Publishing Services, Chennai, India
Printed at Manipal Technologies Limited, Manipal

To find out more about our authors and books
visit www.bloomsbury.com and sign up for our newsletters

CONTENTS

Introduction

Adaptation. is an exceptional film.[1]

I do not mean "exceptional" in the sense of unusually good or outstanding; although there might be a strong case to make for *Adaptation.*'s exceptional quality, that is not the goal of this book. Instead, I mean that *Adaptation.*, a 2002 film directed by Spike Jonze and written by Charlie and Donald Kaufman, is truly an exception in terms of how it works as a film, especially a film produced by a major Hollywood studio and starring A-list Hollywood actors.

One of *Adaptation.*'s many exceptions that this book explores is its relationship to film theory. In most instances, film theory helps us understand a film differently, uncovering new layers, deep structures, and alternate meanings. In some cases, we might contend that film theory is necessary to *truly* understand a film, revealing its power and meaning. But perhaps unique in the context of Hollywood filmmaking, *Adaptation.* actually requires some film theory simply to make sense of it at all, demanding awareness of a theoretical framework to comprehend the narrative and figure out what happens over the course of the film. This book uses an exceptional film to explore a set of critical tools that fall under the broad umbrella of narrative theory, but these tools are just as useful to analyze films that are far more conventional, ordinary, and typical of what Hollywood or other national cinemas produce.

The term "theory" needs a bit of explanation, especially before diving into its exceptional role in *Adaptation.* A theory generally explains something by positing general principles or patterns that are broader than the specific thing being analyzed. For a practical example, you can install a doorknob just by putting the pieces where they seem to belong or following specific instructions that come with the doorknob; however, to really comprehend why the doorknob springs back into place requires an understanding of the physics principle of elasticity, a broader theory that goes far beyond the particularities of doorknobs or even springs. Understanding theories of elasticity could be useful if you want to build your own doorknob either as an amateur or as a professional engineer, or it might be the topic of more abstract research comparing the elastic properties of various materials within different environments. Thus theory helps us move from the particular to the general, and deepens both practical understanding and more abstract analysis.

This is not a book about doorknobs or theories of elasticity. Rather it is a book about film and narrative theory. We can generally make sense of a film's story without any recourse to narrative theory (with the notable exception of *Adaptation.*!), but narrative theory is useful for a deeper understanding of how any specific film might relate to other films or even storytelling in other media. Some narrative theories are useful for analyzing the mechanics of storytelling, highlighting the structures and techniques that are common to a wide range of stories. Other narrative theories help explain the relationship between a specific story and other factors, such as authorship or the process of adaptation. Still other narrative theories aim to understand how the consumers of a story, whether a novel's readers or a film's viewers, comprehend the story being told to them. All of these theoretical topics can be useful for critics striving to understand film narratives on a deeper level, as well as for prospective storytellers looking to apply the insights from such theories in crafting and improving their own film narratives.

This book is a critical analysis of a single film in light of a broader theoretical tradition, not a screenwriting manual for budding film storytellers. However, unlike most works of academic narrative theory, it does consider screenwriting manuals and their various guidelines and principles within its analysis. Thus while it firmly lives within the realm of *critical theory*, with its goals of analysis and examination of existing works, the book explores the related realm of *practical theory*, where such theoretical ideas can be applied to create new narratives. As discussed in Chapter 2, *Adaptation.* is similarly invested in highlighting the role of theory in the creative process, with a prominent work of practical theory serving as a major plot point and a theorist even appearing as a significant character. Thus this book tries to straddle the abstract generalities of academic theory with the grounded particularities of both screenwriting and critical analysis of specific works.

The cornerstones of narrative theory

A central but deceptively simple term in the study of narrative is *text*, which is often used to reference the specific work being analyzed, regardless of medium—a text could be a book, a film, a video game, or a pop song. However, as posited by cultural critic Roland Barthes, the concept of text has important differences from the idea of a *work* of art or culture.[2] While he charts a number of these distinctions, the key difference regards a work as a static cultural object, while a text is a dynamic cultural practice. Considering a film as a static work limits the analysis solely to what appears on-screen within the movie's running time, subjecting the work to a close reading to understand the intrinsic meanings and forms found within. Treating a film as a text considers that its meaning only comes to life through the practice of viewing and thinking about it, and that any critical understanding must be lodged in its contexts of production, reception, and broader cultural circulation. While there are certainly elements of a film that can be examined in isolation from its context, this book embraces a broader sense of textuality where context is always important to understand how films make meaning.

One of the main differences between narrative theory and many other theoretical paradigms that are central to film studies concerns the core question it seeks to answer. The majority of film theories are interpretive, looking to analyze the meanings of a film and connect them to larger cultural issues, such as the representation of gender or racial identities through feminist or postcolonial theories, or the perpetuation of dominant norms and systems of power via the concept of ideology. Narrative theory takes a different approach to studying meaning: instead of asking "What does this film mean?," it asks "How does this film mean?" Such an approach considers how meanings are constructed and conveyed via the design and structure of films and other texts, with primary attention to the patterns of storytelling. Often such an approach is called *formalism*, emphasizing structures and patterns of meaning-making over the meanings themselves.

This is not to suggest that narrative theory is not useful for analyzing the meaning and politics of films or other storytelling media; the core concepts of narrative theory are flexible enough to be integrated into other theoretical traditions to answer a broad array of critical questions. For instance, scholars have married feminist theory to narrative theory to explore how various narrative structures are gendered, such as soap opera seriality or melodrama, provoking emotional responses that are culturally coded as feminine. Likewise, ideology theory often looks at how films reinforce dominant meanings, using narrative theory to understand how plot structures and narrative resolutions work to normalize the status quo and close down opposing ideas or possibilities. No single theory is sufficient to answer all of the relevant questions that a critic might ask of a film, so it is important to be open to combining theoretical models as appropriate to broaden our understanding of any film. But for the purposes of this book (until the conclusion), our analytic toolbox will be limited to narrative theory to understand both its possibilities and limitations to unpacking the ways that films make meaning.

While Chapter 1 explores many facets of narrative theories in depth, most of these ideas are built upon a shared set of cornerstones that are essential to make sense of the entire field. Storytelling is such a universal component of human culture that we rarely stop to think of what we really mean by "story" in exact terms, but narrative theory requires a precise definition of story and its related terms. For a narrative theorist, *story* refers to the narrative world and all that happens within it, including the characters, events, and setting. At one level, this is a commonsense definition—if you try to recall the story of a favorite film, you will probably think about what happens to the characters in a specific setting. Take the example of the classic fairy tale "Little Red Riding Hood," whose story consists of a young girl in the woods bringing food to her grandmother, only to be stalked by a wolf who masquerades as the grandmother, with Red rescued in the end by a hunter. As with most folk tales, there are numerous variations and adaptations that change the story elements: Red might be a girl or young woman, she might be rescued by a lumberjack instead or fight the wolf herself, it might be set in various places and times, and in some retellings Red and the wolf might even enter into an overtly sexualized relationship. These are all changes within the story itself altering what happens within the fictional world, including characters, events, and setting.

However, these are not the only ways that the narrative might be altered. A story is only accessible to us through a specific instance of storytelling, usually called the *narrative discourse*, encompassing the various elements and strategies used to communicate a story. The same story can be told in countless different ways, which greatly impacts what sense we make of a narrative. One could tell "Little Red Riding Hood" solely from Red's perspective, providing insight into her thought processes and limited by her knowledge and experiences, or it could include the experiences of other characters by portraying the encounter between the wolf and grandmother. One could narrate the story chronologically, or jumble the timeframe by starting with Red's discovery of the wolf at grandmother's house, and flashback to her earlier story. A telling might take a long time to portray Red's journey through the woods to create a sense of danger and exhaustion, or simply skip over the travels in a single sentence or film edit. In these various versions, the story remains the same, as the same characters have the same experiences in the same setting, but the storytelling changes dramatically by altering the narrative discourse. One of the central goals of narrative theory is accounting for how different techniques of narrative discourse impact our understanding and the cultural impact of stories.

This distinction between story and discourse are foundational to understanding narrative. Narrative theorist Seymour Chatman offers a succinct summary of this key distinction: "The story is the *what* in a narrative that is depicted, discourse the *how*."[3] Most narrative theory builds upon this crucial differentiation between story and discourse, considering how the telling of a story is distinct from, but interwoven with, the story itself. Such a distinction is best understood in practice rather than abstract theory. Take the popular animated film *Frozen* (Chris Buck and Jennifer Lee, 2013)—as a children's film, it would appear to be fairly simple in its storytelling, aiming to communicate clearly to young viewers. *Frozen*'s story is quite straightforward: Princess Elsa, who has magical ice powers, exiles herself after accidentally freezing her home of Arendelle, leading her sister Anna to venture out to bring her back and save the kingdom. However, the film's narrative discourse is far less conventional than it might appear. The film starts with the girls as children, portraying the momentous events of their childhoods over the course of mere minutes—including jumping forward fourteen years within only four minutes of screen time. Such temporal compression relies upon ellipses in the narrative discourse, cuing viewers to follow the time jumps using storytelling devices like voice-over narration, on-screen captions, descriptive song lyrics, and the rapid aging of the animated characters. This sequence is a clear instance of the difference between story and discourse time, as the characters experience time in a strict chronology, while we are presented only the key moments of their backstory to understand the events that will play out with less compression for the bulk of the film.

The distinction between story and discourse is not just about the use of narrative time, but also includes other facets such as narrative knowledge. Again, *Frozen* provides a good example—one of the film's central storylines is Anna meeting, falling in love with, and getting engaged to Hans, all over the course of one day and a single musical number. When Anna runs off to find Elsa, she leaves Hans in charge of Arendelle, a job that he appears to accomplish effectively. It isn't until the film's climax that we learn of Hans's true motives: he has manipulated Anna into marriage in an attempt to seize the throne. Certainly there were prior moments in the storyworld where Hans's behavior was nefarious, but the narrative discourse withholds sharing such information until Anna herself learns of his deception—while throughout the film we have learned much narrative information about other characters that Anna does not yet know, it restricts our knowledge concerning Hans to what she knows. This revelation is a prime example of how narrative discourse can selectively conceal and reveal story information, highlighting how storytelling manages audience knowledge to maximize dramatic impact. One could tell the story of *Frozen* differently by revealing Hans's treachery early, creating more suspense and anxiety about what will happen when Anna learns of his betrayal—this would significantly change the narrative discourse, and thus our experience of viewing the film, without actually changing anything that happens within the story itself. To effectively analyze a film's narrative, we must always be attentive to how both the story and discourse work both distinctly and in tandem.

There is a third important category of any narrative: its *medium*, or the format that a particular narrative takes. The same story can be told in a wide range of different media, from novel to comic book to live-action film to animated film to videogame. One common tenet of narrative theory is that storytelling is medium independent, meaning that narrative structures and techniques can be used across different media.

This is certainly true to a degree, as a flashback could be used in a comic book just as easily as a film. However, there are some techniques that are more tied to medium; for instance, a first-person perspective takes on a far different effect when you can read a character's internal thoughts in a novel rather than visually representing their experiences in a film. Likewise, a videogame creates an interactive experience where both narrative discourse and story can change in reaction to a player's actions, a facet of storytelling that is not easily translatable to media like television or comics. Thus we need to be attentive to how a narrative's medium helps shape its discourse and the storytelling possibilities that any given medium allows, encourages, or restricts. This attentiveness to medium is particularly important in analyzing an adaptation, as the shift from a book to film involves choices and transformations that can be directly impacted by the dual narrative media, as is directly portrayed within *Adaptation*.

One of the medium-based elements that is particularly central to the study of film is the role of time and temporality as a dimension of storytelling. Every narrative has multiple layers of temporality that correspond to the three categories of story, discourse, and medium. *Story time* is the temporality as it occurs within the storyworld, which is typically linear and chronological; unless time travel is a facet of a particular storyworld, characters experience their universes as a string of moments one after another without interruption or repetition, just as we do in our everyday lives. *Discourse time* is the temporal sequence, duration, frequency, and selectivity as presented in the storytelling, not as it is experienced by the characters. Virtually every film involves compressions in the discourse time by eliminating moments via ellipses and selective presentation—these can be broad reductions, as with *Frozen* compressing fourteen years into minutes, or typical editing patterns that present only the key moments and events in a narrative to maintain interest and active pacing. Some films play more overtly with temporality, such as *Pulp Fiction*

(Quentin Tarantino, 1994), whose discourse time is nonlinear, jumping around between plotlines and perspectives with some repetition and one overt flashback. However, the film's story time remains straightforward, commencing twenty years before the main action in a flashback to Butch's childhood when he received his father's gold watch, and ultimately concluding with Butch and Marcellus escaping captivity—these two scenes are presented back-to-back in the middle of the movie, highlighting the film's atemporal sequence. When watching *Pulp Fiction* for the first time, it is unclear precisely what the story's linear chronology might be, but viewers do attempt to piece together a coherent storyworld that fits together logically; rewatching the film results in even more coherence as patterns and continuities emerge, allowing viewers to draw connections and chart chronologies.

One of the main distinctions between literature and screen-based media like film and television is how they treat temporality in the third level of medium. The time it takes to consume a book is quite variable and idiosyncratic to particular readers, as we all read at different paces and might sometimes reread sections or take lengthy pauses between chapters. Film and television are much more uniform in how viewers consume narratives, leading to particular norms of *screen time* structured by the medium. Film traditionally has been viewed within a strict temporal structure: scheduled by cinema screenings and running straight through from start to finish. The rise of DVDs and streaming in the 2000s has transformed the norms of screen time, as viewers can now watch films on their own schedules, as well as pausing, rewatching, and skipping around in a manner more comparable to reading a book than traditional cinema screenings. However, screen media are still more regimented by length, with norms of feature film duration that are much more prescriptive than lengths of books, and films are still designed primarily to be viewed straight through in a single sitting much more than most other media.

Narrative theory and *Adaptation.*

Even with these core elements of narrative theory in hand we are still not ready to analyze *Adaptation.*, as the film requires a more in-depth understanding of some specific theoretical aspects of film storytelling. The next chapter provides that account, focused on four major facets of narrative theory.

The first section expands on the different paradigms of *practical theory versus critical theory*. While the latter is the standard approach we think of under the banner of academic analysis, applied by scholars to analyze a text, the former is quite important in the realm of film practice. Theories of cinematic narrative are studied and implemented by filmmakers via the popular genre of screenwriting manuals, arguably the most high-profile and widespread use of narrative theory in any medium. If we view critical narrative theory as the parallel to theoretical physics and its concept of elasticity, then applied practical theory corresponds to engineering springs and doorknobs, and thus it is useful to consider them in tandem. We can trace the tradition of practical narrative theory back to Aristotle, and explore how recent applications of practical screenwriting theory approach film structure, characterization, narrative events, and the use of narration, especially in the prominent work of Robert McKee. This mode of practical theory is vital to understand *Adaptation.*, as McKee is the theorist most cited throughout the film, even appearing as a character who emerges as a guru to help the film's protagonist, Charlie Kaufman, navigate his crisis into the film's climactic conclusion.

Another aspect of narrative theory crucial to this topic is found in the film's name: the practice of *cinematic adaptation*. While traditionally adaptation theory has focused on issues of fidelity and comparative norms of medium in adapting fictional novels or plays to the screen, recent developments in adaptation theory have expanded the discussion to include the role of cinematic style, the adaptation of nonfiction sources, and issues of reflexivity in adapting material. All of these are vital issues to understanding *Adaptation.*, which is (at least on one level) an adaptation of Susan Orlean's nonfiction book, *The Orchid Thief*, and is also a reflexive dramatization of the process of adapting a book to film. In considering the particular challenges found in adapting descriptive prose to the screen, we can better understand how films can function as their own distinct medium, even when adapting stories first presented in a written medium.

The third theoretical topic addresses theories of *authorship*. Film studies has long considered the director of a film to be an authorial figure, following the influential auteur theory of the 1950s and 1960s. Both directors and screenwriters can be posited as authors within film, looking at reflexive markers that foreground authorial presence within a film and cue viewers to focus on particular types of authorial figures. In understanding the cultural role of authors, the concept of the implied author is useful to help viewers make sense of a film's narrative design through the positing of a guiding authorial figure; again, the overt presence of authorial figures, both real and fictionalized, in *Adaptation.* encourages us to employ such theoretical tools in making sense of the film.

The final theoretical realm considers the role of *narrative comprehension*, exploring how viewers make sense of a narrative unfolding on-screen, drawing from theories of cognition and perception to account for the viewer's activity in decoding the images and sounds they encounter. To understand how we make sense of even the most straightforward narratives, we need to grapple with cognitive theories of narrative comprehension, focused on perception of temporality, characters, narrative causality, and focalization. Cognitive theories are also useful to understand the role of reflexivity in narrative comprehension, considering how viewers process a film that calls attention to its own storytelling mechanics via the concept of the operational aesthetic.

With these four major facets of practical theory, adaptation, authorship, and narrative comprehension in hand, we will finally be able to dive deeply into *Adaptation.* in Chapter 2, trying to understand a film that marries narrative experimentation and convention, and uses theoretical ideas both within the story and as part of its storytelling design. Hopefully by exploring the film's unique techniques and approach, we can see *Adaptation.* as both exceptional and the exception that helps prove the rules, demonstrating the broad utility of narrative theory.

Notes

1 Throughout this book, I refer to *Adaptation.* with the included period in its title. While this is unusual and looks a bit odd in print, it is the official title of the film as it appears in the credits. See Jeff Scheible, *Digital Shift: The Cultural Logic of Punctuation* (Minneapolis: University of Minnesota Press, 2015), for an interpretation of the meanings of the film's titular period.

2 Roland Barthes, "From Work to Text," in *Image-Music-Text*, trans. Stephen Heath (London: Macmillan, 1978), 155–64.

3 Seymour Chatman, *Story and Discourse: Narrative Structure in Fiction and Film* (Ithaca, NY: Cornell University Press, 1978), 19.

CHAPTER ONE

Narrative theory

No single chapter could cover the full breadth of narrative theory, as it has a tradition as long as any field within the humanities. Instead of touching on every topic of potential interest to film critics and viewers, this chapter will take its cue from *Adaptation.* by foregrounding the specific issues that are most pertinent to understanding the film. Due to that emphasis, numerous key topics are not covered here in depth, many of which could be relevant to *Adaptation.* and certainly are useful for studying film, including genre, beginnings and endings, focalization, spatial narration, and temporality. However, these four key facets should provide a sufficient introduction to narrative theory as to orient the field, and provide a roadmap to analyzing the film in the next chapter.

Practical theory's Aristotelean roots

Few narrative theorists would regard "practical theory" as an appropriate subtopic for the field, nor a worthwhile priority to emphasize over some of the topics that this book mentions only briefly. Certainly the exceptional content of *Adaptation.* drives this choice, as practical theory is a major presence within the film and vital to make sense of its unfolding story. But there is great merit to consider the role of practical theory within a more academic discussion of storytelling and film analysis. Practical narrative theory, primarily in the form of screenwriting manuals and instruction, pervades the filmmaking process, and thus most popular films have been influenced by the lessons and guidelines of such applied narrative theory. Even when considering an unconventional innovative film that seems to break rules in original ways, the specific rules that it breaks were probably codified within a screenwriting manual at some point. Thus practical theory matters in our critical understanding of films, and the links between practical and critical theory can help explain the role of theory in broader terms.

Even though they rarely frame the discussion in such terms, nearly every overview of narrative theory highlights the importance of one work of practical theory: Aristotle's *Poetics*. Known as the oldest extant work of literary theory, *Poetics* is concerned with ancient Greek tragedy and poetry, with a particular focus on what good tragic drama should do, as the opening sentence makes clear: "I propose to treat of Poetry in itself and of its various kinds, noting the essential quality of each; to inquire into the structure of the plot as requisite to a good poem; into the number and nature of the parts of which a poem is composed."[1] In this quotation, it seems clear that Aristotle aims to engage with poetry from both a critical descriptive angle, exploring its "structure" and "nature of the parts," and from a practical prescriptive approach, highlighting elements required "as requisite to a good poem." *Poetics* was not written as a book manuscript, but rather as a set of notes complementing his lectures at his Athenian school, The Lyceum; as such, we might imagine such lectures as ancient prototypes for the screenwriting seminars of today, with Aristotle teaching his followers how to create and appreciate the ideal forms of drama and poetry.

Like most examples of practical theory, *Poetics* offers a taxonomy of elements essential to good storytelling, and presents them as timeless principles of quality and effectiveness. In his categorization of the six key elements of tragedy, he argues that plot (or "the arrangement of incidents") is paramount, with characters coming second. The interplay of plot and characters is central to all practical theories of film storytelling, with screenwriting manuals debating the relative emphases on the actions in a film versus the people who perform those actions. For Aristotle, the structure of the actions is the key to determining whether a drama is successful, with a need for one action to follow another with a clear causal logic of necessity, rather than coincidence, randomness, or divine intervention. Centrally, Aristotle emphasizes that a well-designed plot possesses organic unity, with a clear tripartite structure of beginning, middle, and end—a principle that has been hugely influential to screenwriters in pursuit of a perfect three-act structure.

Poetics is focused on tragedy, with particular actions marked as important within the overall tragic plot structure. One crucial moment is the Reversal of the Situation, where a character finds their fate or situation transformed in a dramatic fashion—such a reversal is a common moment within screenwriting manuals, functioning as a complicating action, turning point, or climactic beat to set up the narrative resolution. Aristotelean tragedy also requires a moment of Recognition, where the hero realizes their own downfall and eventual fate. While few films are structured as tragedies in the strict Greek model, most screenwriters follow Aristotle's general approach of designating specific moments and actions as key points of transformation or plot development, often termed *beats*. Additionally, Aristotle's terms of "complication" and "denouement" are still used to label stages in a film's dramatic structure, even if the specific usage of the terms differs from the Greek tragic model. Many screenwriting manuals draw explicit links to Aristotle's time-honored structures and terms; whether these are accurate updates to his tradition, or just claims to historical legitimacy, matters less than the overarching shared commitment to the usefulness of breaking down a story into clear structures, functions, and moments of dramatic transformation.

Aristotle's discussion of character is harder to adapt to the context of film, as Greek tragedy focused exclusively on noble aristocratic characters of good virtue who fall from grace and suffer; few films share such a narrow scope of potential main characters. But some of his general principles have been influential to filmmakers, such as Aristotle's emphasis on character consistency in action throughout a drama rather than focusing on characters who change drastically, or the need for dramatic characters to feel true to life. One important but subtle Aristotelian principle is his emphasis on partial rather than well-rounded characters—he argues that a drama should present a unified plot, but not attempt to represent a fully unified character. Instead, dramas should present a partial representation of a character as necessary for the plot, but leaving the character's broader range of attributes undramatized and left to the audience's imagination. We can see this principle in practice with films where characters appear to be true to life, but we know only limited information about them, making them intriguing figures within the dramatic action.[2]

Aristotle's arguments about plot structure and character are the most relevant to film, much more than his discussion of poetic diction and song, which are unique to the form of Greek theater, or his influential discussion of the emotional responses of fear and pity, which apply particularly to the genre of tragedy. Nonetheless, Aristotle's approach to drama and storytelling has been hugely influential to the structure of film narrative conventions, forging a path that lives on centuries later.

The practical theory of screenwriting

Certainly many practical theories help shape filmmaking, ranging from aesthetic norms of composition and perspective influencing cinematography, to theories of sound design impacting films' sonic approaches, but no type of practical theory is as widespread and well known as the narrative theories that underlie the dozens of screenwriting manuals that have directly influenced filmmaking in Hollywood and beyond. Many of these manuals position themselves as direct decedents of Aristotle, citing the Greek philosopher to show how their contemporary principles are grounded in ancient wisdom. A prime example of a well-known screenwriting guide that draws links to Aristotle is Robert McKee's *Story*—I single McKee out here both because his in-depth book and associated seminars have been hugely influential to Hollywood screenwriters, and because his book and seminar are prominently featured in *Adaptation.*, and thus serve as the film's central reference point for practical theory.[3]

The most well known and influential element of practical film theory is the three-act structure, adapting Aristotle's breakdown of beginning, middle, and end anchored by dramatic turning points. Although its formulation predates him, this structure was popularized by Syd Field, whose 1970s book *Screenplay* is one of the most referenced of all screenwriting manuals. Field adds to Aristotle by assigning fairly rigid timings for the three acts, with the first act setting up the dramatic situation over the first quarter of the film, the second act complicating the action for the middle half the film's running time, and the final act resolving the drama over the film's remaining quarter.[4] Field's ¼–½–¼ timed model has been regarded as a bible for Hollywood filmmaking by many, with some producers reportedly assessing a new script by flipping to the twenty-five- and eighty-page marks to judge the effectiveness and proper pacing of the turning points between acts, rather than reading the script from start to finish.

Such a rigid formulation of a three-act structure highlights one of the curious aspects of Hollywood filmmaking: every film must feel fresh and new enough to inspire audiences to come see it, but it must also follow enough conventions and formulas to create efficiencies in film production and simple ways to market the concept to potential viewers. Establishing specific timings for the three acts is a production efficiency, allowing producers to evaluate a script quickly and ensure that new stories follow successful precedents to minimize risk. It is also clearly a formulaic pattern that can potentially curtail originality and creativity, mandating a rigid structure that certainly does not fit every story or style of film. Other screenwriting manuals offer variations on Field's three-act mandate; Robert McKee suggests that "the three-act design is the minimum," allowing for the potential of four or more acts as the story demands, although he still contends that three acts is the normal default, with subplots used to enliven the second act.[5] Film scholar Kristin Thompson contends that most Hollywood films actually follow more of a balanced four-act structure, with the traditionally long second act divided into two segments of complicating action and development, sandwiched between set-up and resolution acts, all of approximately equal lengths. She recognizes that Field's structural theory still matters for most screenwriters, but that they organically divide up the long middle act by adding an important dramatic turning point that is best understood as another act break in the middle of a film.[6]

This attention to plot structure pervades nearly all practical narrative theory, with a recent focus on specific beats, the pivotal dramatic events that anchor the story. Blake Snyder, whose 2005 book *Save the Cat!* has become highly influential within Hollywood, builds on the three-act structure to iterate fifteen specific story beats that a script should hit, with specified page numbers for each beat to create an ideal pacing allegedly applicable to any film. By highlighting beats like the Theme Stated (when a character voices the film's underlying theme in the first five minutes), Catalyst (that launches the main story in the first act), and All Is Lost (when the situation is bleakest near the end of act two), Snyder provides a template that he insists is essential to a well-crafted film, and certainly has been highly influential in twenty-first-century Hollywood. Of course, such a highly regimented template provokes critiques of privileging formula over creativity, although Snyder defends his practical theory as parameters to allow creative work to thrive.[7] Snyder's approach is particularly focused on the commercial facet of screenplays, as he contends that hitting the beats is crucial for screenwriters to successfully sell their work; this is quite different than Field and McKee, who highlight their aesthetic ties to Aristotle, but all practical theories of film aim to strike a balance between commerce and creativity.

Beyond the macro-structure of dramatic acts and Snyder's more detailed beat sheet, practical theory also tackles the structure of events within individual scenes. For McKee, "A scene is a story in miniature, . . . unified around desire, action, conflict, and change."[8] Each scene is expected to advance the overall plot as well as standing on its own as a dramatic segment, driven by character goals and emotional stakes; McKee contends that each scene must cause some dramatic change, functioning as a turning point within the overall plot. Such an insistence makes sense in a script where forward plot momentum is a central appeal, but it does raise the question of how films might feature moments of texture or style existing apart from plot, a facet of filmmaking more common to art cinema rather than Hollywood genre movies. Again, the commercial dimension of filmmaking privileges a tightly constructed story over more experimental variations that challenge the primacy of plot, and this emphasis is reflected in the most influential screenwriting manuals.

While most practical theorists follow Aristotle's emphasis on events and plot over character, screenwriting manuals also pay quite a bit of attention to the role of character in film storytelling. The primary principle most theorists emphasize for effective characterization is that the protagonist be goal-driven, and that the film's plot follows the motivation of the main character. As McKee writes, "The energy of a protagonist's desire forms the critical element of design known as the Spine of the story," with other story elements flowing from this core.[9] The protagonist's goal and desire can be conscious, as with most crime dramas, or unconscious, as with many romantic stories, or quite often both, where their realization of what their true desire is becomes a core component of the narrative. McKee offers a succinct summation of the core spine of dramatic storytelling, building on his focus on goal-driven protagonists: "For better or worse, an event throws a character's life out of balance, arousing in him [*sic*] the conscious and/or unconscious desire for that which he feels will restore balance, launching him on a Quest for his Object of Desire against forces of antagonism (inner, personal, extra-personal). He may or may not achieve it."[10] While McKee admits this formulation is an oversimplification, it does help focus both writers and critics on the core essence of a story, and highlights the dramatic engine that moves the narrative forward.

Successful characterization in film does not require creating a fully rounded human being, but rather a figure who serves the purposes of the narrative with some key elements. Beyond being goal-driven, main characters should be empathetic, promoting audience engagement in their emotional journeys and quests—even if they are not likable people, viewers need to care enough about them to spend two hours watching their stories. Characters should be credible per their genre—a character in a parodic farce does not need to be as deep and emotionally complex as the hero of a social drama, but she must act within the story consistently and per that character's specific role, not just to serve an individual joke. McKee emphasizes that films reveal characters by what they do, via actions witnessed on-screen, rather than through inner monologues or soliloquies, devices more common to literature and theater respectively. In fact, we often know more about characters through their actions than their claims about themselves, which are often masks of self-denial and rationalization. Thus any distinction between events and characters is somewhat of an analytic convenience, as we cannot truly experience an action without the people involved in it, nor characters without the things that they do.

Most of these aspects of practical narrative theory focus more on story rather than narrative discourse, highlighting what happens to whom in a film rather than how the film communicates that story to viewers. Plot structure is a by-product of both story and discourse, as the pacing of an inciting incident and narrative climax is dependent on the pacing of discourse time, rather than the experiential chronology of the storyworld—the filmmakers must choose which moments to portray or skip within the discourse, even though the characters experience much more over the course of the story, and those experiences rarely match the timing of a film's act structure. These decisions of inclusion or exclusion, portrayal or omission, all impact not only the pacing and rhythm of a story and its ability to adhere to the ideal act structure of conventional films, but also the balance of knowledge between characters and audiences.

Every film contains gaps between what viewers know and what various characters do, and these gaps are established by the narrative discourse. We are rarely inside the heads of characters, and even when we do hear their thoughts, we lack the wide range of memories and story experiences that occurred offscreen. Some information is equally unknown to both characters and viewers, most typically the future events of the narrative—when watching a film, we want to know what will happen next, prompting *curiosity* toward events and concern for the well-being of characters. McKee suggests that curiosity and concern come together to create *suspense*, a prime storytelling drive, whether within the high-stakes world of thrillers ("Will the killer strike again?") or the lower-stakes genre of romantic comedies ("Will the couple get together?"). Often, characters know more than viewers, creating a sense of mystery as to what key information is being withheld from us ("Which of these characters is really a spy?"). Other times, a film uses *dramatic irony*, sharing important knowledge that a character does not know, leading us to anticipate what will happen when the information is revealed ("How will she react when she discovers that her husband is a spy?"). All of these variations of narrative knowledge are important tools in a filmmaker's toolkit, constructing a narrative discourse that manages story information to create viewer engagement, interest, and emotional connection.[11]

Managing story information can connect directly to character as well, with narrative knowledge aligned to a protagonist. McKee calls this "point of view," although that term confusingly also refers to a specific camera angle—a more general term is *perspective*, indicating whose experiences are matching our own.[12] Managing narrative perspective is a balancing act: the more that the narrative discourse is restricted to the protagonist's perspective, the deeper the emotional connection will be to that character, and the greater the potential for mystery and suspense concerning the actions of other characters. But the freedom to present information that the protagonist lacks can make narrative exposition much easier, raise the opportunity for dramatic irony, and allow viewers to feel connected to other characters as well.[13] As per the example in the Introduction, *Frozen* (Chris Buck and Jennifer Lee, 2013) shares narrative information broadly, presenting story moments aligning with the experiences of Elsa, Anna, Kristof, and Hans, as well as a more depersonalized omniscient position; the use of musical numbers convey a sense of emotional interiority, as with Elsa's revelatory song "Let It Go," creating the impression that viewers are fully knowledgeable of the relevant story information. The moment where Hans's true motives are revealed, we are surprised not only by this story information, but also by the realization that we were actually seeing Hans solely through Anna's narrow perspective, as the discourse restricted our knowledge without signaling that restriction. Such manipulations of knowledge and perspective are important tools for filmmakers to leverage the particular cinematic devices of visual and sonic storytelling, versus the interiority accessible via the written word.

Screenwriting manuals focus less on specific techniques of atypical narrative discourse, like flashbacks or voice-over narration, than more conventionally straightforward dramatization of events and characters. However, they do highlight that such devices need to serve the core dramatic drive of a film, rather than serving as a crutch for exposition or manufactured intrigue. One of the mantras of virtually all screenwriting guides is "show, don't tell," foregrounding the visual nature of filmmaking; McKee clarifies this phrase to suggest that it is not just the difference between words and images, but it is crucial to present exposition through dramatic moments and scenes. By making the exposition part of the drama, we come to care about the story information along with the characters, and pick up crucial information without being bored by its presentation. McKee notes that films should play to the medium's strength of dramatic presentation rather than narrated explanations, else "the film becomes little more than multimillion-dollar books-on-tape, illustrated."[14] Such a need for medium specific techniques becomes particularly essential when dealing with this book's second major facet of narrative theory: adaptation.

Theories of adaptation

The goal of practical theory is to guide filmmakers in their creative process, and as such there are certainly manuals offering advice for adapting literature and other media to the screen. McKee briefly tackles the problem of adaptation, arguing that films need to play to their visual nature and ability to "dramatize extra-personal conflicts" on a larger scale than novels and theater.[15] For the screenwriter, the goal of adaptation is to capture the spirit of the original source by reinventing the story and its telling for the cinema, not to be slavishly true to the novel or play; McKee warns that a source that is too "pure" to its original medium is hardest to adapt, as the narrative spirit is too embedded within the original's form to suit the externalized drama of film. However, this is where we reach the limits of practical theory—McKee and others aim to help writers create new cinematic works, while critics are invested in analyzing the works that already exist. McKee's guidelines for adaptation have little to teach us about the film *Adaptation.*, except to suggest that perhaps *The Orchid Thief* would be an inappropriate book to adapt for the screen. To understand the broader terrain of cinematic adaptations, we need to look at critical narrative theories.

Just as practical screenwriting theory is best understood within the context of the commercial film industry, much of the academic work on film adaptation is forged by its specific contexts. The scholarly field of film studies developed in large part out of literary studies departments, such as English Literature in the United States and Great Britain; many early academic critics who wrote about film were trained in studying literary forms, and expanded their horizons to include cinema. Thus much work within film studies, especially in its early decades, foregrounds the relationship between film and literature, particularly in cases of adaptation. Such work also privileges literary sources of film adaptation, particularly the novel and theater, over other potential sources, like historical nonfiction, comic books, journalism, games, or television programs. Emphasizing literary adaptation not only built on the scholarly expertise of many critics, but also helped to legitimize film in the eyes of academic traditionalists, who had long been quite skeptical of the worthiness of studying commercial popular culture. Hollywood also uses literary adaptations to boost the medium's cultural legitimacy and garner recognition, with scholars focusing on such cases for similar reasons.

It would be an overstatement to suggest that adaptation is a major area of narrative theory; rather it is a topic that is often mentioned without much theoretical grounding. In large part this is due to the adaptation studies falling in the gap between literary and film studies, and not prompting much in-depth theoretical work from either discipline, neither of which seems to want to claim primary custody of the topic. As one of the few scholars who has explored theories of film adaptation in depth, Thomas Leitch suggests, "Adaptation theory has remained tangential to the thrust of film study because it has never been undertaken with conviction and theoretical rigor."[16] Thus instead of outlining primary theoretical concepts, debates, or approaches to adaptation (as they arguably are not sufficiently developed to explore), this discussion of adaptation studies surveys some topics relevant to the area and highlights relevant concepts, but without the depth that other topics in narrative theory warrant. Adaptation studies are linked to a more pervasive theoretical concept of *intertextuality*, which considers the web of relationships between multiple cultural works, including allusions, short paratexts like film trailers and posters, sequels and remakes, and parodies. Like all intertextual connections, adaptations require us to consider multiple texts within their potentially varying cultural contexts, and thus cannot be studied in isolation from broader practices and circulation.

One of the major topics for adaptation studies is the issue of *fidelity*, where critics judge an adaptation primarily on how well it captures the original source material. Since the question of fidelity is typically posed by critics whose primary allegiance is to literature, often the answer is automatically assumed to be negative, highlighting how films inevitably fall short in meeting the standards of the literary original. Film scholar Robert Stam convincingly shows how the question of fidelity uses language that is often "profoundly moralistic, rich in terms that imply that the cinema has somehow done a disservice to literature."[17] Stam goes on to show how the default preference for the literary is based upon a number of biases and prejudices that value older forms more than newer media, privilege language over images, and assume that the comparative accessibility of cinema over literature makes it less aesthetically rich and complex. Nearly every recent work of adaptation theory spends a moment dismissing fidelity as a critical dead end, before moving on to consider the more nuanced issues involved in adapting source material for a new medium.

However, we should not ignore issues of fidelity entirely, but rather reframe the question. Instead of considering fidelity as a moralistic question of quality, where the original is inherently superior to the adaptation, we can frame fidelity as one of the issues that filmmakers wrestle with when adapting from another text. We can categorize films on a spectrum from close to loose adaptations of the original—close adaptations aim to retain as much of the story material as possible from the original source, whereas loose adaptations more freely add new elements or discard original material. Consider two film adaptations of the Jane Austen novel *Emma*, released one year apart: Amy Heckerling's *Clueless* (1995) loosely adapts the novel, shifting the setting to contemporary Beverly Hills and significantly changing nearly every character name, event, and relationship, while Douglas McGrath's *Emma* (1996) offers a close take on the novel, retaining its era, location, characters, and most of the plot. This is not to suggest that *Clueless* is the less successful film, as its greater popularity and reputation suggest otherwise, nor even that it is a less successful adaptation; instead, the film was far less interested in representing the novel rather than using its themes and insights as a launchpad for a new transformative take on the material. Questions of fidelity matter in understanding these two films, but less as a marker of quality than as part of the strategies that different filmmakers use to pursue an adaptation with widely divergent results.

Close versus loose is one simple way to view the relationship between an adaptation and its source, but numerous scholars have offered more fine-grained taxonomies of adaptations as part of intertextual practices. Probably most detailed is Thomas Leitch, who suggests ten different ways a film might approach its source that map across the close to loose spectrum. A *celebration* valorizes the original by maximizing fidelity, while an *adjustment* makes it more appropriate for the screen via compression, expansion, updating, and/or superimposition onto another text. An *imitation* transposes the original time and place, but in a way that attempts to use the original's essence to shine a light on the new setting, whereas a *revision* attempts to recast how we understand the original text by transforming its spirit. *Colonization* borrows the original's reputation but relocates it into radically new contexts of nation, genre, or tradition; an even more radical approach is *deconstruction*, which reflexively highlights its own status as adaptation as part of its transformative impulse toward the original. An *analogue* uses loose reference to a source for thematic resonance and parallels, but does not import plot, characters, or setting directly; a *parody* might directly reference an original, but uses the reference as a point of mockery or humorous parallel, rather than sincerely trying to retell its story. Even more distant from original sources are *secondary imitations*, which adapt adaptations themselves, and thus have multiple sources to draw from, and might even multiply into deeper levels of reference by being further adapted themselves. Finally, *allusions* are the most common realm of intertextuality, referring to other texts without any claims for fidelity or direct adaptation—and yet, Leitch suggests, can provide key references for plot structures and characterizations, like with the ubiquity of the Oedipus myth or Cinderella story. These ten modes of intertextuality need not be exclusive, as a single film might embrace any combination of them, but they provide a useful categorization of how originals and adaptations might potentially connect.[18]

In considering the relationship between a film adaptation and its original source, we should think carefully about what elements of the original are being adapted via any one of these strategies. Typically, fidelity refers to story elements like narrative events, characters, and setting, where viewers experience the fiction constructed in a novel recreated on-screen. But as narrative theory teaches us, story is only one realm of narrative, with the narrative discourse serving as our way to access the storyworld and events. Total fidelity to a source's narrative discourse is nearly impossible when switching medium, as the norms and possibilities of cinematic storytelling are quite different than literature or theater. We might consider an unabridged audiobook to be a faithful adaptation of a novel's narrative discourse, but even then the performance of the narrator could be more or less true to the fiction's written voice—perhaps a film where each page of a novel were shown on screen for a minute would be the ultimate in adaptation fidelity, but clearly a failure as a film. Clearly full faithfulness in narrative discourse is not the goal, as even adaptations that are faithful to a source's story may be critiqued for being insufficiently cinematic, overly literary in tone, or too "stagey"—all instances where fidelity to an original's narrative discourse is seen as a failure of adaptation. Thus we need to look carefully at what it means to transform a narrative discourse into film, and how it shapes how stories are told.

Adaptation, medium, and narrative discourse

While there are whole genres of books that use images, like graphic novels, picture books, and textbooks, most literature that spawns film adaptations uses a single channel of verbal communication nearly exclusively, save for the few novels that use occasional illustrations, page design, or fonts to convey meaning. Films have quite a bit of verbal communication as well, including on-screen text via captions, or shots featuring a letter or sign to be read by viewers, and most commonly, the spoken word. For a literary adaptation, one of the core questions is how best to capture the original's use of language within the film; dialogue is the most straightforward way to retain the original language, as with Shakespearean adaptations putting the poetic language into the mouths of characters, even when the film changes the time frame and setting from the original. However, dialogue that reads well on the page might fall flat when spoken in a film, and much of what might be conveyed via dialogue in the theater might be better served by wordless visualization on the screen. Much depends on the qualities of the original source—novelist Elmore Leonard is well known for his distinctive ear for dialogue, so strong adaptations of his work like *Jackie Brown* (Quentin Tarantino, 1997) or *Out of Sight* (Steven Soderbergh, 1998) succeed in large part by retaining his unique verbal style, but many other novelists whose dialogue is unremarkable might not inspire attention to the use of language as a core goal of an adaptation.

Novels that rely upon descriptive prose or the voice of a narrator as a defining element pose more of a challenge in adaptation. *Voice-over narration* is the most obvious solution, a device that can allow literary prose to be presented in a film, but one that prompts controversy among practical and critical theorists alike. Similar to the stance of practical theorists like McKee, critical theorists have long been skeptical of voice-over as a non-cinematic device, one that privileges "telling" over "showing," and thus runs counter to the visual essence of cinema. For such critics, voice-over is typically a weak form of adaptation that fails to visualize the story effectively, but instead borrows the legitimacy of literature and uses the shortcut of description as exposition. However, Sarah Kozloff offers a compelling defense of voice-over narration, highlighting how this dismissive attitude stems from the origins of cinema as a silent medium, leading critics to mistakenly privilege image over sound as the essence of filmmaking. She contends that branding voice-over narration as an inherently literary device is off-base, as it ignores the performative and time-based aspects of voice-over, and how it can successfully interact with visuals to produce uniquely cinematic storytelling. Kozloff argues that we must analyze voice-over narration on its own terms, whether in an adapted or original story, exploring how it can work as an element of cinema rather than just a literary by-product.[19]

When literary adaptations do not use the original's words via voice-over, dialogue, or on-screen text, they still often aim to retain the prose's tone and style via evocative use of visuals and sound. This is a rich area of adaptation criticism, examining the specific ways that cinematic style and form can work to match the tone, mood, and emotional response of a literary source. Often filmmakers endeavor to render a richly described storyworld via sound and image, as with Peter Jackson's highlight successful adaptations of Tolkien's *The Lord of the Rings* trilogy (2001–03), which were nearly unanimously embraced by fans of the original books for how well the films created an evocative visualization of Middle Earth and its inhabitants. Since many of the pleasures of Tolkien's novels, and the broader fantasy genre that he helped create, stem from such detailed world-building, the films' success depended on creating a credible and compelling on-screen version of that world, where the representations are not only true to Tolkien's descriptions, but also provoke similar emotions of awe and wonder as captured in the books. Adaptations in other genres may be less dependent on world-building, but focus more on creating characters that are equally engaging as the original versions, as with various film and television versions of Sherlock Holmes that aim to create vivid on-screen renderings of the iconic detective via well-crafted performances, dialogue, and plotting. Such comparative accounts of original and adaptation are less driven by a formal set of generalizable theories than the specificities of criticism and in-depth analysis.

There are some formal elements of filmic adaptations that do connect to broader theoretical concepts, especially around the issue of medium specificity. The concept of *medium specificity*, which has a long history within art criticism and aesthetic philosophy, asserts that any specific artistic medium has certain properties that define it—as Siegfried Kracauer states in the opening sentence of his landmark book *Theory of Film*, "This study rests upon the assumption that each medium has a specific nature which invites certain kinds of communications while obstructing others."[20] For adherents to this assumption of medium specificity, the study of adaptation can identify the particular ways that each medium shapes the narrative and how filmmakers overcome the obstructions that their medium poses in adapting literature. Seymour Chatman exemplifies this approach in his instructively titled essay "What Novels Can Do That Films Can't (And Vice Versa)," where he analyzes the distinctly different strategies of description and perspective within literature and cinema. Chatman concludes his essay with a summation of this approach: "Each medium has its own properties, for better and worse usage, and intelligent film viewing and criticism, like intelligent reading, needs to understand and respect both the limitations these create and also the triumphs they invite."[21] Thus we need to be attentive to how choices that filmmakers make are not just broad sets of creative options, but constrained by the limits and possibilities of their medium.

A good example of such constraints involves the use of description. Take the instance of a new character's introduction in J. K. Rowling's book *Harry Potter and the Prisoner of Azkaban*; she describes the first glimpse of Remus Lupin on the train as follows: "The stranger was wearing an extremely shabby set of wizard's robes that had been darned in several places. He looked ill and exhausted. Though quite young, his light brown hair was flecked with grey."[22] This brief unremarkable description seems to be fairly neutral and visual in a way that would convey itself well to the cinema—it is not a subjective account of his appearance, nor one relying upon uniquely literary devices. However, it still relies on elements that are distinct to literature: the brief description directs our attention to particular elements (the places the robes had been darned, the flecks in his hair) that convey elements of his personality, while leaving other facets of his appearance unremarked upon, such as the color of his robes and whether Lupin has facial hair or glasses. Likewise, describing him as "ill and exhausted" suggests a level of interpretation at work, as there is no explicit visual marker that indicates such traits—implied in this phrase is that the stranger struck Harry Potter as ill and exhausted, as the book is narrated from Harry's perspective. When visual elements are communicated via words, they inevitably direct our attention to particular elements, ignore other features, and invite us to interpret and judge what is being described.

Compare this description to Lupin's introductory moment in the film version (Alfonso Cuarón, 2004), where he appears on the train as Harry awakens from a Dementor attack. Lupin's appearance is consistent with the written description, but simultaneously more and less specific—his robes are unremarkable, with no clear signs of being darned or shabby, and any gray in his hair is imperceptible. However, we see a much more fleshed out visual perspective of him, identifying the color of his wardrobe and skin, establishing his facial hair, and seeing how he holds his body and moves. While many of these descriptive elements are parsed out throughout the book, cinema's visual dimension requires such details to be shown all at once, for when we see a character, we see most of his physical attributes simultaneously. Additionally, it is unclear that the filmic Lupin looks ill and exhausted, as our attention is rather focused on Harry looking ill and exhausted after his Dementor encounter, and thus Lupin looks healthier by contrast. There are certainly cinematic ways to convey Lupin as unhealthy, but the necessity to present the narrative efficiently led the filmmakers to compress this moment into the forward-moving plot, rather than linger on Harry's perception of this stranger. These two moments across media certainly present the character somewhat differently, but both communicate the core idea of Harry's first impression toward Lupin: this man does not look like a typical Hogwarts professor, setting up a surprise when he is revealed to be just that. Per Chatman's approach, we should regard these two moments not by valorizing one over the other, but by looking at how each utilize the norms and possibilities of their medium to effectively communicate the narrative moment. We should also recognize the cultural impacts of such medium norms, as illustrated by another *Harry Potter* character: when a black actress was cast as Hermione Granger in the stage performance of *Harry Potter and the Cursed Child*, some fans decried the choice as unfaithful to the books. However, author J. K. Rowling responded that the books describe Hermione's eyes, hair, and teeth, but never specify her race or skin color, highlighting how the absence of descriptive information in literature often leads readers to fill in their own details following dominant social norms, but film and theater cannot leave such details unmarked.[23]

Not every critic embraces this theory of medium specificity. Thomas Leitch criticizes Chatman for assuming that any medium has an innate essence that dictates what it can and cannot do, a position that many scholars equate with the idea of technological determinism.[24] Leitch and others highlight that while a medium does have technological elements that matter, such as cinema's combination of moving images and sound versus literature's words on a page (or potentially, screen), we should not assume that those properties determine their usage. Instead, a medium's communicative practices are shaped by the interactions between technologies, creators, consumers, and various historical contexts—at any given time, there are norms for how films might tell stories, but these are less essential to the medium than tied to that specific context.[25] We only need to look at how radically different filmmaking strategies might be used in contemporary Hollywood versus 1980s India versus 1950s France or any other specific context, to acknowledge that the "essence" of the cinema is not forged by timeless intrinsic properties, but the particular historical circumstances that shape the production of specific films. Nonetheless, we can take a more contextualized view of medium differentiation by understanding how a specific adaptation works within the particular contexts of both the original and film versions, and be attentive to how the creative choices were shaped by the norms of each medium within those contexts.

While there are numerous other interesting topics within adaptation theory, one is particularly important for the case study of *Adaptation.*: the role of nonfiction as source material, since the film's source text is the journalistic book *The Orchid Thief*. Every film based on a true story as its source material can be seen through the lens of adaptation, ranging from documentaries adapting the experiences of their subjects to biopics focusing on the life of a real person, to the vast realm of historical fiction that uses real events as the setting for an original story. Adapting factual material where there is a clearly identifiable source in the form of a nonfiction book resembles the process of adapting a fictional original, as the filmmakers must make similar choices as to what source elements to include, such as individual characters, particular events, structural elements like chronology and narrative perspective, and specific language. Many nonfiction books are not structured like narrative films, lacking clear dramatic turning points and unambiguous goal-driven protagonists, and many contain vast amounts of description and analysis that seem ill-suited to the screen. Thus the process of adapting a nonfiction book to a dramatic film typically involves imposing dramatic structure on real events and simplifying the messy contours of real life, prompting the hybrid genre to often be referred to as docudrama.

An interesting and well-studied example of nonfiction adaptation is *JFK* (1991), Oliver Stone's exploration of President Kennedy's assassination and the conspiracy theories around the murder. The film is credited as based on two books, *On the Trail of the Assassins* by Jim Garrison and *Crossfire: The Plot That Killed Kennedy* by Jim Marrs; Garrison's book is the most direct source, as Garrison himself is the film's protagonist and the film's cowriter Zachary Sklar had worked with Garrison on the book. Marrs's book forms less of the film's narrative than offering some of the arguments concerning the assassination that the film's dramatizes. In adapting the nonfiction material, Stone and Sklar certainly deviate from both the books and the factual record, inventing some characters and events, as well as compressing chronology to maximize the dramatic impact of the story. Of course, these source materials themselves have controversial claims for truth value, as both books posit that the officially sanctioned story of the assassination is a lie and offer different versions of what they each believe really happened—in this way, these books also function as interpretations that adapt the evidence they found into a narrative account of events, making the film a secondary imitation in Leitch's terms, as it adapts works that already are adapting material. While *JFK* is an extreme example, it highlights how all factual material is also interpretive, and that the adaptation of a nonfiction source is always working at a significant remove from the real historical events that are being represented.

Dramatic adaptations of nonfiction can easily get wrapped up into ethical issues, as real people and events are portrayed on-screen in ways that may be more or less truthful, flattering, or appropriate. When tackling historically significant events and people, filmmakers generally are willing to be critical of public figures and people in power without fear of litigation or ethical breach, but filmmakers generally strive to be more ethically concerned about dramatizing figures outside the public eye or lacking the power to defend themselves. A film that adapts a published nonfiction source has paid for the rights to the story, and a coterie of lawyers have approved the stipulations that typically give the filmmakers the right to represent the source material however they wish. But even as filmmakers might choose to be more or less deferent to their nonfiction subjects, they must also consider their ethical obligations to their audience—by claiming that a film is "based on a true story," they should bear in mind that viewers might assume that everything represented on-screen is basically true, if not in the precise sequence of events but in the spirit of what occurred. In tackling a nonfiction source, the concept of "fidelity" bears additional weight, as the original is not just the creative work of a writer but often the real lives of actual people. This weight of responsibility is carried by the film's author, a role that is quite complicated in any film but additionally so in an adaptation—to understand film authorship, we need to add another key set of theories to our toolbox.

Defining film authorship

Certainly questions of authorship have been far more central to film theory than issues of adaptation, even though they are intimately connected. Adaptation criticism that is invested in notions of fidelity typically assumes authorial value as tied to the literary original—a Shakespeare play or Austen novel should be faithfully adapted out of respect and admiration for the genius of the original author. Notions of authorship in film have been adapted from their literary origins, complicated by the industrial and collaborative practice of film production, but still invested in the core belief that artistic value typically emerges from the creative inspiration of an individual author. Thus as film studies struggled to become a legitimate academic field and subject of serious critical writing, one of the central ways that critics posited the value of both the medium and their critical own insights was to identify the authorship of films.

Filmmaking is inherently a collaborative process requiring many participants in the various stages of preproduction—writing and planning, production shooting and performing, and postproduction—editing and sound mixing. There is no single individual who can take credit for this entire process, and most filmmakers will attest that dozens of people add their creative input to the finished product. However, a number of critics in the 1950s and 1960s argued that the filmmaking process was ultimately authored by each film's individual director, an approach commonly known as the auteur theory, as argued in the French film magazine *Cahiers du Cinéma* and later reasserted in the United States by the critic Andrew Sarris. These critics identified how film directors working within industrial systems like Hollywood could still produce films with unified styles and themes, suggesting that true auteurs can rise above the collaborative system to function as authors. While this approach to authorship drew upon the legitimacy and unified creative vision implied by literary authorship, the auteur theory acknowledges that a film's director is part of a collaborative and institutional system. If the literary writer is ultimately celebrated for *authorship by origination*, assumed (however erroneously) to have written every word as an individual, a film's director is granted *authorship by responsibility*, ultimately making the necessary creative choices by supervising and guiding all of the film's many collaborators, even if much of the specific work was done by others.

The auteur theory emerged out of film criticism written for cinephiles in specialized magazines and general interest periodicals, not the realm of academic theory. However, its privileging of directors as the primary creative force in filmmaking had a profound influence on academic film criticism and theory. Many landmark works of film scholarship of the 1970s and 1980s focused on single directors to organize their studies, even when their primary theoretical concerns were shaped by other approaches like psychoanalysis, formalism, or semiotics. In contrast, virtually no scholarship focused on the other creative participants in the filmmaking process, such as screenwriters, producers, cinematographers, or composers, while studies of actors focused more on their cultural role as stars than their creative work as performers. In university curricula, courses frequently centered around single directors such as Federico Fellini or Ingmar Bergman, paralleling the pedagogical focus on authorship typical of literature studies, although it was never the screenwriters who were accorded this authorial attention (except for cases where directors also write their films). Thus even if early film studies did not necessarily generate much scholarship around theories of authorship, it was implicitly invested in the theoretical idea that a film's director functions as its author, and should be studied as the key creative figure.

There is a notable lack of scholarship on screenwriters as authors per se, especially when compared to the widespread circulation of practical theory that frames screenwriting as the originating site of film storytelling. In 1975, film critic Richard Corliss wrote a book analyzing screenwriters as film authors, inspired by the landmark auteur studies of the era, but virtually no critics or scholars have followed Corliss's critical lead.[26] The one notable exception of a screenwriter gaining attention as an object of critical inquiry is Charlie Kaufman, whose screenwriting work has been the subject of numerous articles and books—as discussed in the next chapter, there is little doubt that Kaufman's decision to place himself as the on-screen protagonist of *Adaptation.* has contributed to his presence as the exceptional case of a screenwriter who is accorded authorial status.[27]

What is the role of an author in the study of film? An authorial figure is generally used in service to other theoretical paradigms and core research questions. Thus psychoanalytic film studies investigates how films can express and reveal aspects of the unconscious, and often map those desires and repressed urges onto an authorial figure, especially one whose films play with psychosis and desire, such as Alfred Hitchcock. Formalist critics are often interested in compelling uses of visual and sound style, and thus a particularly distinctive author, from Orson Welles to Wes Anderson, can be used to define the parameters of close analysis and identify individual distinctiveness. Critics invested in understanding how films might perpetuate or challenge representations of identity might analyze the politics in the films of a director from a traditionally marginalized group, such as gender in Agnes Varda's films or race in the work of Spike Lee. Dozens of film studies books are framed as single-author studies of a director, but nearly all of them use that authorial figure as a case study to follow other methodological concerns and approaches, or offer a critical biography, interweaving the events of a director's life with their filmmaking.

For narrative theorists, authorship could help define a case study to consider the particular storytelling techniques practiced by an individual filmmaker. For instance, nearly all of Stanley Kubrick's films are adaptations of novels, covering a wide range of genres, national origins, eras, and subject matter. One could analyze the particular narrative strategies that his films use to adapt fiction, considering if there are particular unifying techniques that make a Kubrick adaptation distinctive.[28] A more contemporary example is Christopher Nolan, who has made many films that fall under the label of "puzzle film" or "narrative complexity," with unconventional use of temporality, multiple dimensions, or shifting perspectives. A narrative analysis of Nolan's work might compare his "complex" films such as *The Prestige* (2006) and *Inception* (2010) with his more conventional Batman films, looking for both commonalities and differences within his storytelling techniques.[29] In these and other narrative analyses, authorship serves as a way to define the scope of analysis, allowing the analysis to search for patterns that make a given director distinctive within their filmmaking context.

Authors and narrators in film storytelling

No matter what theoretical school one uses to analyze film, one common idea that pervades much critical analysis invokes the author as the intentional agent behind a film. The notion of *authorial intention* has been long debated within both literary and film studies, trying to understand whether a text's meanings are determined by what its creator aimed to communicate. Notions of authorial intent map onto a spectrum, ranging from strong intentionalists, who believe that a work's core meaning is defined by what its creator intended to express, to anti-intentionalists, who contend that once a text is created, the author's role is complete and the text can be interpreted and understood in a variety of ways with no correspondence to intentionality. Most critics fall somewhere between these poles, acknowledging that films are created with particular intents and goals in mind, but that their finished forms allow for a broader range of possible meanings and interpretations than the author intended. One useful concept is that of "design" over intent: filmmakers design a film to convey certain ideas or impacts, but its meanings will frequently surpass or even contradict that design, depending on the viewer's contexts or perspectives on the material. Regardless of how much weight you put in authorial intent, there is no doubt that notions of authorship can be useful to understanding a film and its design.

Discussions of authorial intent highlight how the role of the author can remain relevant long after the creative process that produces a film. Authorship is a concept that viewers frequently evoke as they are watching and thinking about a narrative, so narrative theory has developed some useful, although controversial, terms and models for how authors factor into the understanding of stories. Most of these concepts derive from literary theory, where the identification of an author is less of an issue than for film, leaving critics to debate the function of the author in the process of consuming and interpreting stories. When we read a novel, we are usually quite aware of the author, often thinking about what they intended, how it connects with their other works, and how the writing fits into their particular style and voice. Especially for prolific authors, each new book feels more like you are reading the author rather than a book—thus you might say you're reading "an Agatha Christie mystery" or "the new Stephen King," where the author's name stands in for the individual work.

Literary theorists recognize that our knowledge and assumptions about Agatha Christie matter as we read her fiction, but are not identical to the real person; thus they developed a useful distinction between the biographical author and the implied author. A *biographical author* is a real person who (presumably) wrote the book, with all of the experiences, contexts, and internal thoughts that add up to a person's life. The *implied author* is how a reader understands the creator in relation to the text, both in their knowledge of the biographical author and the assumptions they make about authorial intent while reading a book. Thus when I read an Agatha Christie book, I construct a figure in my mind of the book's author, based on my limited knowledge of Christie as a real person, as well as my experiences reading her other books; as I try to solve the mystery as I read, I engage with this implied author figure to imagine "What might she be doing?" in trying to mislead me or play with my expectations. Whether or not you believe that a biographical author's intent is the ultimate meaning of a work, it is commonplace to imagine an author during the reading process and try to parse out "What does she mean?" and "How does this fit with her other works?" as you read and think about a narrative.

When we invoke an implied author in the process of consuming a narrative, we are not limiting our engagement to the individual text itself. Authorship is part of an intertextual web, where we draw upon our knowledge of a wide range of materials both created by and referencing an author. The author's name operates as a placeholder for an array of references: other works she has written, interviews she has given, our knowledge of her life, images we have seen of her, and commentary and criticism we may have encountered about her work. Thus the implied author is not detached from the biographical author, as it is forged from the material that a real author has produced; however, it is much more variable and idiosyncratic, as any given reader has a different array of authorial knowledge to draw from when constructing their own particular implied author figure. This is why your impressions of your favorite author differed greatly from the first book of theirs you read, when your knowledge and assumptions about the writer were probably quite limited, to the last one you have read, as your intertextual connections and expectations have grown to significantly shape how you approach any new work of theirs. This intertextual cluster of knowledge, assumptions, and connections is what Michel Foucault terms "the author function," with the author's name serving to define, evaluate, contextualize, and help interpret a work.[30] When we imagine an implied author while reading or interpreting a book, we are drawing upon the author function to help construct this figure and attribute creative intents to it.

The implied author is particularly prominent when a story features *unreliable narration*, where the narrator is misleading readers in crucial ways. In literature, the narrator is the figure who tells the story, and instances of first-person narration embed that narrator as a character within the story. An unreliable narrator presents story information and perspectives on the fictional world that we call into question; even though such a narrator is our only window onto the fiction, we can detect their unreliability by the information they present that we know or suspect to be false (within the storyworld), based on both real world knowledge and other characters' behaviors. But in recognizing that the narrator is lying to us, we need another point of reference in the storytelling where we can locate the intentional act of constructing this unreliability—this is a function of the implied author. We attribute the intent of a fiction to the implied author, placing them on a higher level of knowledge and awareness than the narrator, whether reliable or not, and thus can recognize a difference between the character narrating the story and the authorial figure who has created both the story and the narrating character. Thus in Mark Twain's *The Adventures of Huckleberry Finn*, we read Huck's first-person narration as the thoughts of a young character who admits to lying and clearly sees the world in a self-centered way, and thus attribute the construction of this deceitful character and the stories he tells to our concept of Twain as implied author.

Such constructions of unreliable narrators, implied authorship, and the author function derive from literature, where authorship is clearly marked on a book's cover and creativity is assumed to be singular; however, things become more complicated for film. First off, the very concept of a "narrator" is hard to identify in most films—there is no communicative voice telling the story as there is in a novel, as a film's story is told via the multitude of visual, sonic, and structural elements of filmmaking rather than the comparatively streamlined model of the written word. Even a film that has an explicit "narrator" conveying the story via voice-over is rarely positioned as the agent behind the images and sounds that unfold in the film, as the vocal narration functions more as yet another sonic filmmaking element, whether that narrator is a character in the film or an offscreen "voice of god" framing the narrative. Although there is some debate among scholars, most view cinematic narrators as a less-than-useful concept, and instead suggest that the film effectively "narrates itself," conveying its story information through images and sounds.

Unreliable narration in film is comparatively rare, as we assume that everything we are seeing and hearing is "real" within the film's fictional world. Films that do feature unreliable narration typically make it part of a narrative twist, where it is eventually revealed that what we had seen had been misleading in some way. Sometimes that revelation is grounded in a framing narrative, where an on-screen character has been telling the story that we have seen dramatized in the film, as with the misleading flashbacks in *The Usual Suspects* (Bryan

Singer, 1995); in such instances, the unreliable storytelling is built into the film's fictional world itself, as we see the lying character telling the untrue story from a point within the narrative's reality, and only the dramatized flashbacks are untrue. Other cases are trickier, as the film's storytelling is not framed by a point of reference outside the deception, but rather the visual and sonic elements represent some aspect of reality that misleads viewers. Often this involves the status of particular characters, where how we perceive them does not fit with how everyone else in the storyworld does: not to give away their relevant twists, but *The Sixth Sense* (M. Night Shyamalan, 1999), *Fight Club* (David Fincher, 1999), and *A Beautiful Mind* (Ron Howard, 2001) all portray their storyworlds and characters in ways that mislead us to thinking that what we are seeing is "real" within the storyworld, rather than through the skewed and unreliable filters of particular characters. Yet in each of these films, we can attribute the unreliability to the film itself as narrator, rather than needing to imagine a narrating character who is actively deceiving us—even in *Fight Club*, where a character's voice-over does filter the storytelling, it does not feel like that character is generating the film's images and sounds in the same way that a literary narrator seems to be producing a book's words as the narration.

For such cases of unreliable narration, thinking about authorship helps us understand how a film's storytelling works, but in complicated ways. As discussed above, the collaborative process of producing a film makes the identification of a singular individual as the site of intentionality and creativity tricky—the process of attributing a film to a director is a key rhetorical part of the author function, as naming an author helps delimit the text. However, many casual viewers are unaware of a director's identity on most films, and thus might be less likely to invoke an implied author while watching it. Take beloved American film classics *The Wizard of Oz* (1939) or *Casablanca* (1942): how many of the millions of viewers who have watched these films could identify Victor Fleming or

Michael Curtiz as their respective directors? If you don't know who directed a film, does that mean you are not engaging with an implied author while watching it?

This question is debated within film studies, as some scholars doubt the overall usefulness of the implied author as a concept. Leading narrative theorist David Bordwell argues that the implied author is "an anthropomorphic fiction" that obscures the fact that the film text and its narrational system tell the story, and there is nothing to be gained by creating a hypothetical author figure to anchor that storytelling.[31] Seymour Chatman disagrees, as he notes that an implied author provides a convenient shorthand to attribute the storytelling to a human agent, even though that person is not equivalent to the real biographical author.[32] We can take this usefulness a step farther by connecting the implied author with the intertextual web of knowledge that viewers have around the author function—when we imagine a film's narrative as being constructed by its director, we can augment that understanding by drawing upon what we know about that director and their other films. Thus in the case of *Casablanca*, a viewer who knows other films by Michael Curtiz or something about his biography will link that knowledge to their construction of Curtiz as the film's implied author, attributing choices and meanings to him. For viewers who don't know anything about Curtiz, or may not even know the name of the film's director, a generic implied author figure can serve as the locus of the film's intent—when you watch the film and wonder "Why did they put the flashback to Paris so late in the film?," the implied author is the "they" that you imagine having made that decision. Since creativity is a human act, the implied author can be a more organic way to think about intentionality and choices than the impersonal concept of a film's narrational system.

An implied author may not be an essential construct for every film, but some seem to demand such a concept. Films where the authorial figure is also its star personalize the notion of authorship, and often encourage us to look for connections between the character and creator, as with Woody

Allen's *Annie Hall* (1977) or Clint Eastwood's *Unforgiven* (1992). In such instances, it is hard to depersonalize the film's storytelling because its authorial figure is prominently featured on-screen. Other directors, such as Alfred Hitchcock and Quentin Tarantino, often appear via on-screen cameos in their films, as well as offering a distinctive set of stylistic and thematic commonalities that encourage us to regard their films as distinctly authored. Coupled with a film industry that heavily promotes authorial identity, we are encouraged to engage with such films using an authorial figure in our viewing process, personalizing questions of intent and design, such as "What is Tarantino trying to say about race in *Django Unchained* (2012)?" or "How is Hitchcock creating suspense in *Rear Window* (1954)?" Such questions, which regularly come to mind when watching such films, is the implied author at work, connecting a strong directorial persona and distinct filmography with our need to attribute narrative choices to some decision maker. As we will see in the next chapter, this process is particularly crucial for *Adaptation*.

As with literature, the concept of an implied author helps make sense of unreliable or misleading narration. In *The Sixth Sense*, the final minutes reveal that the film has misled us, portraying events in such a way that encouraged particular assumptions about characters and certain relationships. We are never cued that our perception is filtered through other characters and their understanding of the storyworld, so this twist's revelation makes us rethink how the story had been told, a reconsideration that attributes this clever deception to the film's previously unknown writer/director M. Night Shyamalan as the implied author. The surprise success of *Sixth Sense* established Shyamalan as a prominent authorial figure, fueled by his cameo appearances in his films and interviews where he promoted his own talents and influences; his subsequent few films all ended with narrative twists, creating his authorial signature that grew to eclipse the perceived quality of his films. In watching Shyamalan's later films, the expectations of narrative twists and a somewhat dour psychological tone framed what viewers expected from his films, making the surprises overly predicable. The downward arc of his career is a testament to the power of implied authorship in setting expectations, guiding viewer reactions, and impacting narrative possibilities—it is difficult to make sense of how viewers turned against Shyamalan's films without embracing the concept of the implied author as part of narrative consumption.

Cognitive comprehension

As the discussion of the implied author suggests, the process of understanding a narrative can be more complicated than it might first appear, and thus has prompted scholarly attention to develop theories of narrative comprehension. This process may seem obvious, given that mainstream cinema strives to make its stories as clear as possible—why do we need a theory to explain how we comprehend narratives, given that it's a process that every film viewer or reader knows how to do? One reason is that some narratives (including *Adaptation.*) are much more challenging to comprehend, so we cannot just rely on the seeming obviousness of making sense of a story. But even seemingly straightforward stories require a fairly complex set of practices to follow, so theories of narrative comprehension help us understand what we all do every time we watch a film. Such theories not only shine a light on how we follow more complex narratives, but they are useful for aspiring filmmakers to help understand the processes of comprehension that their viewers would follow in making sense of their stories.

Most analyses of narrative comprehension draw upon cognitive science, a school of psychology focused on mental processes. Cognitive film theory can explore a number of issues, ranging from how we transform the flickering light on a screen into mental representations of people and places, to how films trigger emotional reactions in viewers. Cognitive narrative theory considers the mental processes by which a viewer takes in a film's images and sounds, constructs a mental image of a coherent narrative world, and understands the story events as they unfold over time. Such an approach presumes that viewers engage with a film via both conscious and preconscious processes, but not with the unconscious sublimated desires or associations argued by psychoanalytic critics—at its core, cognitive film theorists assume that the act of watching a film is a rational activity that is best accounted for by this theoretical approach to mental processes, not by a more interpretive approach to the unconscious. Thus as referenced in the Introduction, such an approach is less invested in what a film means, than how it conveys meanings to viewers.[33]

A core concept of cognition is the use of *schemata*, the repeatable routines of mental processing. Think of what happens when you look at a book—you perceive a pattern of light, dark, and color that your brain categorizes as a tangible object (as opposed to a photograph of a book), as a specific type of object (differentiated from other types, such as food or living creatures), and as written language signifying ideas. These are all automatic, repeated preconscious schemata that you cannot choose to ignore: can you see this sentence as a series of graphic lines that do not signify words and ideas? If you can read English (which presumably you can), it is virtually impossible to view these symbols as anything other than language, because you have learned the relevant schemata to perceive and comprehend such writing. Even if you do not know Portuguese, looking at Adaptação still probably makes some sense because of its similarities to English; however, Адаптация probably does not automatically get processed as a meaningful word (unless you have learned to read Bulgarian), although you probably assume it is language given the presence of symbols that resemble A, T, N, and R. The symbols 適応 are even less obviously a word (unless you read Japanese), as the symbols do not correspond with English or other alphabetic languages, although the context of this paragraph would certainly lead you to hypothesize both its linguistic function and meaning. เมื่อปราศจากบริบท การระบุคำว่า’การปรับตัว’นั้น แทบจะเป็นสิ่งที่เป็นไปไม่ได้ในรูปประโยคนี้.[34]

This example of reading multiple languages highlights the various types of schemata that we use to process information. Some schemata are ingrained, preconscious processes, such as perceiving patterns of light as representing the physical world, that are virtually universal to all able-bodied people; the ways that people with disabilities differ from such baseline processes can highlight the cognitive and physical operations that we take for granted in both everyday life and storytelling. Identifying this object as a book relies on *categorization schemata* that are learned through experience—at some point in your childhood, you acquired the category of "book" to differentiate such objects from "toy" or "box," and later developed finer-grained categories such as "hardback" versus "paperback." Even though this category schema is learned and nonuniversal, as there are certainly some cultures that do not have books, it functions automatically and preconsciously, as you are not aware of your categorization process nor can you choose to not perceive it as a book. Other categorization schemata are conscious, as you need to actively discern whether this book is fiction or nonfiction, what it is about, or whether you have read it before. The more knowledge and expertise you gain about a topic, the more detailed such categories can become, as you recognize authors, genres, publishers, and formats to understand this object as a very specific type of book; if you are trained as a graphic designer or printer, you might categorize other elements like fonts, paper type, and binding method that untrained eyes would simply overlook.

Language comprehension is a much more complex set of learned schemata, involving categorical recognition of individual letters, symbols, and words, procedural combination of those units into meaningful phrases and sentences, and contextual connections between words, meanings, and broader knowledge and assumptions. For your native language, you probably have no memory of acquiring such schemata, but learning languages as an older child or adult highlights how much work it is to acquire such abilities. Yet once you have learned a language, it becomes automatic and preconscious—if you can read Japanese, you cannot help but perceive 適応 linguistically. Both visual and linguistic cognition are key processes in understanding a film, as we are constantly processing the images we see and sounds we hear into coherent concepts of people on-screen and spoken dialogue through automatic preconscious schemata. For instance, when the patterns of light and sounds from the film portray a character's mouth moving and the sounds of spoken words, we automatically presume that the character is speaking in a manner parallel to the experiences we have when talking with a real person, even though the images and sounds were captured at another time and place highly distinct from our everyday conversational experience. While such preconscious cognition forms the basis of cinematic comprehension, narrative analysis focuses more on higher levels of cognitive processing while watching a film, exploring how we make sense of different elements of film storytelling through a mixture of automatic preconscious and more variable conscious processes.

Making sense of characters

One key aspect of understanding a film narrative involves understanding characters. We certainly can identify the images of actors as distinct people in a film using mostly the same visual and verbal schemata as we do in real life, but it takes more to recognize and comprehend them as characters. As discussed earlier with practical theory, creating engaging characters is a key task for any storyteller, so they rely on existing norms and contexts to help us figure out who people are and what role they serve in a narrative. Whenever we see a person on screen, we quickly gather information about them to help situate their narrative function—are they there as the protagonist, the villain, a sidekick, a cameo role, or a background extra? Much of that contextual information comes from the film itself, as the character's actions and dialogue, how people react to her, how she looks, and how she is framed on-screen, all help us establish her importance and narrative role. A large team of creative personnel work to make each actor's appearance and performance fit with the film's designed construction of their characters, tapping into the often preconscious mental associations that viewers will make the first time they see a character on-screen.

We also bring a wide range of information from outside the film to bear on our identification of characters, such as broader narrative norms and patterns tied to specific genres or contexts. One of the most important contexts that viewers reference in making sense of characters is the actor's previous roles and *star persona*: when you see Tom Cruise on-screen, you immediately bring to mind his cluster of performances and your offscreen knowledge about him, which guides how you interpret his new character. If you have any passing knowledge of Cruise's star persona and acting history, you probably assume he will be the film's protagonist, and that he will accomplish his goals with a mix of physical prowess, charm, and arrogance. Your particular opinions about a star like Cruise might vary greatly from other people's attitudes, but there are enough broadly circulating assumptions and meanings tied to any high-profile star to make that actor's reputation and history important to how films construct and convey meanings concerning their performances. Thus star personas and broader extratextual knowledge of actors form important schemata that both shape how producers construct characters and guide viewers' processes in comprehending a film.

The most basic aspect crucial to understanding a character is *recognition*, identifying a figure and situating their role within the film. Sometimes recognition is more complicated than simply connecting a face to a name and a narrative function, as with the uncommon cases where one actor plays multiple characters in a film—such characterizations require us to actively track which character is speaking at any given time, and parse the links between the multiple characters as part of the narrative's meaning. One more common complication is when a character is a real-life person, as with historical dramas or other nonfiction adaptations. In viewing nonfiction characters, we bring another set of assumptions and knowledge to bear on the character, judging the character's appearance against the real person, and trying to understand what events and traits are truthful versus fictionalized. Of course, some films represent more well-known true characters than others, which skews how we engage with their representations: Steven Spielberg's film *Lincoln* (2012) represents dozens of true characters, but most viewers will regard the protagonist Abraham Lincoln with a broader set of assumptions and points of reference than more historically obscure (yet equally "real") figures like William Bilbo or Elizabeth Keckley. Additionally, more prominent figures will likely have been represented many times in various media, creating a library of references that factor into our perceptions and judgment of "accuracy" in such characters. Thus we process an iconic character like President Lincoln by comparing any one on-screen representation to what we already know about his history and the other representations we have seen in various media, while we treat previously unknown figures more as film characters without such preconceptions to draw upon.

Recognition is one of three facets of comprehension that Murray Smith has outlined as the core way that we engage with characters in films.[35] The second is *alignment*, which concerns the range and depth of knowledge that we have about various characters. Not all characters are treated equally by a film's narration—some films restrict our knowledge to information that only one or two characters know, while others are much more wide-ranging in their access. This can be dependent on genre, with mysteries often restricting our knowledge to what the detectives learn versus romantic comedies that tend to share access more broadly across a range of characters. Additionally, films can provide greater or lesser depth of character knowledge, ranging from a surface understanding of external actions and dialogue, to more interior access via voice-over, subjective visuals as with fantasy sequences, or other devices to take us inside a character's head. Processing and keeping track of such character information usually occurs beneath the level of our awareness, as filmmakers are quite adept at providing sufficient cues and guidance about who knows what within a film; in fact, it is only when a film stumbles in providing the necessary cues that we become aware of the challenges of tracking character information, as we consciously begin to wonder about characters' knowledge, distracting us from the more engaging process of following the narrative.

One of the key outcomes of processing character information and alignments is the third of Smith's trio of character facets: *allegiance*. One of the primary ways we engage with a film is rooting for certain characters to succeed and others to fail in their goals, and thus filmmakers need to cue us to have differing allegiances toward characters. Alignment is a key factor in guiding allegiance, as the more we know about a character's interiority and the more time with spend with her, the more likely we will want her to succeed in her goals. Likewise, a character who is obscure, opaque, or enigmatic will garner less sympathy, as we cannot understand their actions and motivations. Allegiance is often tied to moral judgment, as you evaluate a character's goals and actions based on your own sense of right and wrong that transcends a film, and thus we process what we say in the film by categorizing events via moral evaluations. Filmmakers recognize the role of morality—the title of the influential screenwriting manual *Save the Cat!* refers to a stock moment in a film where the protagonist performs an unquestionably noble action, such as rescuing an endangered pet, that endears them to the audience.

In a film with more complex characters and a less black-and-white sense of morality, part of a viewer's engagement involves adjusting our allegiance as we discover and witness morally ambiguous behaviors, challenging our clearcut sense of morality. As a time-based medium, our engagement with characters changes over the course of a film, as we gain more knowledge of their behaviors and beliefs, see them interact with others, and watch them work toward their goals. This can be even more pronounced in a film franchise, as with our changing moral perception of Severus Snape in the *Harry Potter* series as we learn more about his backstory and his secret agreement with Professor Dumbledore. Such an example highlights how adaptations can alter our allegiances as well, as viewers who have read the source material will bring additional character knowledge that may not be known by novice viewers, or that may even end up cut from the film version—Snape's character is much more developed in the books, and thus readers who are watching the films are likely to have more sympathy for him as carrying over from the originals rather than viewers who know only what is revealed in the film.

Over the course of any film or series, viewers need to manage a vast array of character information concerning actions, memories, desires, relationships, goals, deceptions, and unknown enigmas, usually covering a cast of a dozen or more significant individuals with varying levels of alignment. Such character comprehension is one of the major cognitive processes involved in watching a film, combining conscious and preconscious schemata in a generally smooth system of tracking and organizing characters that we rarely pay attention to. In this way, watching a film is a surprisingly intensive mental process.

Processing norms, genres, and paratexts

Following characters is one of the most important ways that we mentally engage with a film, but there are other key elements we need to process as well. We construct mental maps of spaces represented on-screen, from the micro-spaces of a set, as with the bathroom in *Psycho*'s (Alfred Hitchcock, 1960) iconic shower scene, to the macro-spaces of a fantasy world that spans a multi-film series such as *The Lord of the Rings*. We track chronology of both story and discourse, working to fit together the backstory we learn about, flashbacks we witness, and other atemporal storytelling techniques. We catalog the various information that we learn about the storyworld over the course of the film into our memory, recalling relevant information as needed and referencing other memories of real-life experiences and other cultural texts that seem pertinent to make sense of the unfolding film. Although watching a film might seem like a passive and automatic process that you cannot remember "learning" how to do, it involves a broad array of schemata and mental processes that require constant attention and cognitive engagement.

One way that filmmakers simplify these cognitive processes is by constructing and referencing norms that serve as patterns and shortcuts for viewers. Some patterns are *intrinsic norms*, developed individually by particular films—rules of behavior for a particular storyworld, visual motifs, repeated dialogue moments, stylistic quirks, recurring musical themes, and other patterns of storytelling work to establish shortcuts for how a given film's storytelling works. For instance, a nonrealistic film needs to clarify how its storyworld works differently in this film, as with the particular treatment of time travel in *Back to the Future* (Robert Zemeckis, 1985) versus *12 Monkeys* (Terry Gilliam, 1995) versus *The Time Traveller's Wife* (Robert Schwentke, 2009). A film that uses voice-over narration must establish who the voice is in relation to the story, as with a character directly addressing the camera, as in *Annie Hall*, versus a narrator who is primarily offscreen, as in *The Big Lebowski* (Joel and Ethan Coen, 1998), versus a framing narrative presenting the narrator telling the story to another character, as with *The Princess Bride* (Rob Reiner, 1987). While all of these are particular choices that might be shared with other films, the particular way that a movie sets up its own intrinsic norms is an important way that it guides our comprehension and engagement.

Other patterns work as *extrinsic norms*, common to broader sets of films and other narrative media. Many extrinsic norms are established through the guidelines offered by practical theory—the subdivision of a film into a three-act structure is an extrinsic norm, providing an underlying pattern that helps viewers expect a particular dramatic arc to a story. Character types and relationships are often extrinsic norms, as we rely upon our learned assumptions of how a protagonist or romantic couple are supposed to act as shorthand for processing a film's narrative. One of the most effective ways that a film can create authentic surprises is to establish and then violate a well-known extrinsic norm. For instance, *Psycho* establishes Marion Crane, played by prominent star Janet Leigh, as the film's protagonist for its first forty minutes, before she is brutally murdered in the shower before the film's midpoint. Beyond just its shocking violence and kinetic use of editing and music, much of this scene's power derives from violating our expectations: we fully anticipate following Marion for the rest of the film per all conventions of narrative structure and schemata of character engagement, as well as Leigh's billing as the film's star. Thus extrinsic norms can both be followed to make narrative comprehension more streamlined, and be broken to create storytelling surprises.

One important type of extrinsic norm is *genre*, used to categorize the content, form, and intended reactions to films. Genres certainly guide filmmaking practices—think of how differently the narrative action of somebody getting hit in the head with a hammer would be as represented in a horror film versus a slapstick comedy versus a social drama about labor conditions among construction workers. Genres also guide viewer comprehension, as we bring an array of assumptions to a genre in terms of the film's likely succession of narrative events, what types of characters are likely to appear, and how we are supposed to react to what we see and hear. Whenever we watch a film that seems to clearly belong to a genre, we call up a host of memories and intertextual references that help create shorthands and guide expectations for what we are watching.

Part of the challenge of watching a film without a clear genre identity is that we lack the anchors and signposts typical of more conventional movies—since the narrative is less predictable, we need to pay closer attention to piece together what is going on, and find it harder to anticipate what might happen next. For many viewers, such challenges make an unconventional film more enjoyable and exciting, but often viewers enjoy watching a film whose originality stems more from how it offers subtle variations on or impeccable execution of established norms or genres. We shouldn't privilege one type of film or viewing pleasure over the other, as any one viewer might adore some movies for their unconventional innovations and others for how perfectly they carry out genre conventions and norms. In either case, understanding a film requires viewers to gauge what it strives to accomplish and judge it on its own terms.

One important way that a film establishes those terms is through *paratexts*, the cultural material that circulates in relation to a core text like a film or novel. We rarely watch a film without having our expectations and assumptions framed by such paratexts: we may have seen trailers, posters or DVD covers; read reviews and commentaries; consumed celebrity gossip about the film's stars; heard interviews with the director that establish a particular authorial function; observed social media buzz around the film; or even stumbled across spoilers revealing plot details. All of this material helps establish a web of information and references that become activated when viewing the film—perhaps we anticipate a particular scene or line featured in the trailer, observe a character through the lens of the actor's star persona, or wonder why the film received such strong critical praise or condemnation. Paratexts can function to establish and reinforce norms for viewing a film, as we already have a loose mental map of the film's narrative that we work to expand, revise, or reevaluate as we watch. The broad variety of paratexts that circulate around any given film makes its consumption quite variable, as the particular combination of related paratexts, intertexts, and cultural references that forges people's frames of reference before seeing a film is likely to be unique to each viewer, making it hard to generalize how a film will be comprehended. Nonetheless, there are some common shared processes that are useful to understanding film storytelling.

Thinking about paratexts and norms highlights how each viewer enters into a film from a wide range of positions and contexts, drawing upon varying amounts and types of relevant knowledge and experiences. But film storytelling assumes that the practice of film viewing becomes more uniform once a film begins, and thus creators invest a good deal of creative energy to making sure that a film's opening moments establish the relevant norms, tone, contexts, and approach to the story to ensure effective comprehension—in short, a film's beginning teaches us how to watch the rest of the movie. Often this involves providing important information about the storyworld and backstory, as in the opening crawls offering written story summaries at the start of every *Star Wars* film, or *Casablanca*'s voice-over narration that locates the film's action within the context of Morocco during Second World War and explains how the city of Casablanca functions within refugee transit. Other times, a film's opening throws us directly into a story in progress without much context—aside from an early graphic stating "South America, 1936," *Raiders of the Lost Ark* (Steven Spielberg, 1981) tells us little about who is wandering through the wilderness or why, and it isn't until three minutes in that we see Harrison Ford's face to recognize him as the main character. Instead, this opening establishes norms that the excitement of an action sequence is more important than details about the storyworld or characters, and that we are in for a thrilling ride. Even more uniquely, *Annie Hall* opens with a static shot lasting 1:40 of Woody Allen speaking directly to the camera, telling jokes and offering a meandering set-up of his character's anxieties about his romantic life; this unconventional opening quickly sets the stage for the film's sense of humor, use of direct address, and willingness to embrace unconventional styles and techniques. Each of these opening sequences highlight how films teach us how to watch them in their early moments, establishing norms and styles, conveying relevant narrative information, and providing (or evading) relevant contexts.

Asking questions about story and discourse

When we consume a story, part of our mental activity is positing questions and making hypotheses about the narrative. While we may think that we are fully "in the moment" of a story, we are still projecting forward and backward in our mind, trying to fit the images and sounds we're consuming into a larger narrative pattern. Many of these questions emerge at a preconscious level that we learn to overlook; for instance, when a film dissolves between scenes to relocate the action to a new time and place, a viewer wonders when and where this new scene has taken her. She probably does not notice this uncertainty, as viewers have developed schemata to help process such transitions by waiting until the scene unfolds to reveal its time and place in the story. Viewers make hypotheses in the face of uncertainty as well, following a film's norms to assume the most likely answer—if a character gets into bed for the night, and the film dissolves to a scene in the kitchen with light streaming in the windows, we can presume that the transition took us to the next morning in the same apartment without consciously thinking about it.

It is only when answers to such questions are slow to arrive, incomplete, or contradicted that we tend to notice our own confusion: a new character is introduced without clarity as to their identity, an ambiguous transition does not signal whether the new scene is a character's subjective fantasy or a flashback, dialogue references unknown people and events without explanation. We might make hypotheses about these uncertainties, but if a film refuses to confirm them and resolve the ambiguities, we become consciously aware of what we do not know about the story. If such uncertainties pile up, we may judge the film as poorly made with incoherent storytelling; however, if a film seems to be purposely ambiguous and opaque, as with *Mulholland Drive* (David Lynch, 2001), we might embrace the ambiguity as part of its pleasurable design. How might we judge whether a film is purposely opaque or frustratingly incoherent? Paratexts and norms can help guide such judgments—for *Mulholland Drive*, the category of "art cinema" allows for greater ambiguity, David Lynch's directorial career has long preferred a surreal and uncanny tone over coherent storytelling, and the film's visual and sound style seems to be designed to produce unsettling emotional moments. Thus a viewer watching the film for the first time would probably come to accept that it invites ambiguity and uncertainty within the first twenty minutes or so, eschewing coherent linear storytelling for a more affective experience, or simply turn it off for not delivering the type of narrative coherence we expect from a movie.

We pose other types of questions to understand a film's story as it unfolds, concerning how the narrative events fit together. One crucial type of question and hypothesis involves *curiosity*, looking to fill gaps in a story's past. As we learn information about characters, events, and the storyworld, questions emerge about what has already happened in the backstory—how did these two characters meet? Who murdered the hero's father? What caused this interplanetary war? Such questions provoke curiosity in viewers, with the film prompting us to think about these knowledge gaps before providing the answers. In *Casablanca*, we get numerous references to Rick and Ilsa's past relationship in Paris before the film flashes back to resolve our curiosity. A well-made narrative effectively cues us on which curiosity questions are important to the story—what really happened to Anakin Skywalker prior to *Star Wars: A New Hope* (George Lucas, 1977)?—and which of the nearly infinite bits of unknown information are not worth thinking too much about—who invented R2D2? Fulfilling our important curiosity questions is one of the key ways that we actively engage with an unfolding narrative, as we fill in gaps in our knowledge as the film unfolds.

Most key questions in narrative comprehension are not about backstory but about future events, built around the core driving issue of "What will happen?" Often, we have enough knowledge to predict that something may happen, creating a question of *anticipation*. When a character enters a dark alley where we know a murderer is lurking, we anticipate what gruesome fates might befall him. When characters are engaged in a tension-filled chase, we imagine what calamities might happen to their cars. When a couple goes on a first date, we assess what romantic futures might play out over the rest of the film. This process of anticipating what might come next is one of the most crucial ways that narratives engage us, as we become invested in potential outcomes and dread the worst-case scenarios we imagine. Contexts guide these hypotheses, as genre norms and previous narrative events cue our anticipation and help streamline the comprehension process.

One particular form of anticipation deserves special attention: *suspense*. We often equate suspense with the act of anticipating something surprising, but film scholar Noël Carroll offers a more precise definition: a subset of anticipation hypotheses when the events that viewers hope to happen to characters has a low probability of occurring within the storyworld, and the most likely outcome is highly undesirable for the characters that viewers have strong allegiance toward.[36] When James Bond is trapped by an arch-villain and about to be killed, when a romantic lead discovers that her ex-boyfriend did not receive her love letter and is about to marry another woman, when a murderer is holding the protagonist hostage in a closet while the police search the house—these are all instances of suspense. Importantly, in most such instances, we know that genre norms dictate that the protagonists will actually survive and prevail in these confrontations, but the moral and narrative logics of each film make it feel as if all hope is lost and defeat is inevitable. Such a contradiction highlights how we can engage emotionally with a narrative situation that feels troubling and anxious, even when we are confident that the events that are likely to unfold will turn out just fine.

Questions of anticipation can drive a narrative forward, and we often think that effective stories answer such questions in surprising ways. But surprise is arguably an overrated element of storytelling, as many narrative techniques work directly against surprise: genre norms often dictate a predictable sequence of events, remakes and adaptations often present stories that are well known to viewers, and the prevalence of viewers that seek out spoilers and rewatch films suggests that there are important narrative pleasures beyond surprise. Often engaging with a film involves anticipating what we already know will happen (or are very confident that will happen), by focusing less on what a narrative event might be and more on how the story will be told—watching a horror film, we usually know that a given character will be killed, but we want to see both how the action takes place, and how effective the film is in scaring us despite knowing what will probably happen. This focus on "how it will happen" over "what will happen" is called the *operational aesthetic*, calling attention to the mechanics of storytelling and inviting viewers to pay attention to such narrative machinery and enjoy its craft and creativity.[37] Such appeals to the operational aesthetic are common in many genres where the narrative outcomes are predictable, from historical fiction to romantic comedies to action films, suggesting that a viewer can engage simultaneously with the story events and the narrative discourse telling the story, with both aspects capturing attention and prompting anticipation.

A focus on the storytelling and narrative discourse via the operational aesthetic is one kind of *reflexivity*, where a narrative embraces some form of self-awareness and acknowledges its own artificiality. Like with most narrative elements, reflexivity can come in a range of different varieties and degrees. As discussed earlier, unreliable narration forces viewers to differentiate between the story we are seeing and the storytelling itself, creating one particular form of reflexive engagement. Reflexivity is often used as a comedic device, ranging from characters quickly addressing the audience for a gag, to a complete breakdown of the cinematic illusion at the end of *Blazing Saddles* (Mel Brooks, 1974), where the climactic fight in the parodic Western breaks through the set to reveal the Hollywood studio where the film itself is seemingly being produced. Many films are reflexive in terms of theme, where the narrative action refers to the cinema, either explicitly as with Hollywood narratives *Singin' in the Rain* (Stanley Donen and Gene Kelly, 1952) and *The Player* (Robert Altman, 1992), or via an allegory, like *Inception*'s construction of cinematic dream scenarios or *Rear Window*'s representations of voyeurism as a metaphor for film viewing. Some movies highlight the mechanics of film production in ways that suggest that we are witnessing the creation of the film we are watching—mockumentaries like *This Is Spinal Tap* (Rob Reiner, 1984) or *Real Life* (Albert Brooks, 1979) feature documentary filmmakers as characters, producing the movies we are viewing, while pseudo-documentaries like *The Blair Witch Project* (Daniel Myrick and Eduardo Sanchez, 1999) and *Paranormal Activity* (Oren Peli, 2007) use fictional found footage to suggest that what we are watching was produced by the film's characters. Texts that thoroughly embrace reflexivity are often called *metafiction*, where a fictional work represents itself and its own storytelling as much as presenting a fictional world, making their own narration the subject of the fiction. Nearly every form of reflexivity is on display in the classic animated short *Duck Amuck* (Chuck Jones, 1953), where Daffy Duck spends seven minutes arguing with his animator for how he should be portrayed, leading to a total breakdown of the lines between story and discourse, drawing and reality.

Reflexivity is a fitting final topic for this whirlwind tour of narrative theory, as it draws upon nearly every other concept outlined in this chapter. A reflexive film often engages with its own design and storytelling structure as outlined by practical theory, while differentiating itself as unique by how it violates conventions and typical guidelines as taught by screenwriting manuals. While not all reflexive films are adaptations, most adaptations are at least a bit reflexive in how they acknowledge their own source material and invite viewers to think about the various versions and their differences. Certainly reflexivity calls attention to authorship, as the presence of filmmakers in the story makes an implied author more relevant, as we try to differentiate between the on-screen representations and behind-the-scenes creators. All incarnations of reflexivity invite viewers to think about the dual aspects of story and discourse, calling attention to how films are made and tell stories, while simultaneously encouraging us to become immersed and invested in a story. Reflexive films require a more complex form of narrative comprehension that invites us to pose questions about the relationship between the storyworld and the real creation of the film, and keep various levels of "reality" in mind to make sense of characters and events. As the next chapter explores, *Adaptation.* embraces all of these facets of reflexivity, and arguably extends them further than nearly any other Hollywood film.

Notes

1 Aristotle, *Poetics*, trans. S. H. Butcher (New York: Hill and Wang, 1961), 1.

2 For more on Aristotle's influence on screenwriters, see Kevin Alexander Boon, *Script Culture and the American Screenplay* (Detroit: Wayne State University Press, 2008).

3 Robert McKee, *Story: Substance, Structure, Style and the Principles of Screenwriting* (New York: ReganBooks, 1997).

4 Syd Field, *Screenplay: The Foundations of Screenwriting* (New York: Delta, 1979); for more on the history of the three-act structure, see Kristin Thompson, *Storytelling in the New Hollywood: Understanding Classical Narrative Technique* (Cambridge, MA: Harvard University Press, 1999).

5 McKee, *Story*, 220.

6 Thompson, *Storytelling in the New Hollywood.*

7 Blake Snyder, *Save the Cat! The Last Book on Screenwriting You'll Ever Need* (Studio City, CA: Michael Wiese Productions, 2005). For a critique of how Snyder's beat sheet formula has made Hollywood films overly formulaic, see Peter Suderman, "Save the Movie!", *Slate*, July 19, 2013.

8 McKee, *Story,* 233.

9 Ibid., 194.

10 Ibid., 196–97.

11 Ibid., 346–55.

12 For more on the concept of point of view in film narrative, see George M. Wilson, *Narration in Light: Studies in Cinematic Point of View* (Baltimore, MD: Johns Hopkins University Press, 1986).

13 McKee, *Story,* 362–64.

14 McKee, *Story*, 345.

15 McKee, *Story*, 365–66.

16 Thomas M. Leitch, "Twelve Fallacies in Contemporary Adaptation Theory," *Criticism* 45, no. 2 (2003): 149–71.

17 Robert Stam, "The Theory and Practice of Adaptation," in *Literature and Film: A Guide to the Theory and Practice of Film Adaptation*, ed. Robert Stam and Alessandra Raengo (Malden, MA: Wiley-Blackwell, 2004), 1–52, 3.

18 Thomas M. Leitch, *Film Adaptation and Its Discontents: From* Gone with the Wind *to* The Passion of the Christ (Baltimore, MD: Johns Hopkins University Press, 2007), 93–126.

19 Sarah Kozloff, *Invisible Storytellers: Voice-over Narration in American Fiction Film* (Berkeley: University of California Press, 1988).

20 Siegfried Kracauer, *Theory of Film* (Princeton, NJ: Princeton University Press, 1997, originally published in 1960), 3.

21 Seymour Chatman, "What Novels Can Do That Films Can't (And Vice Versa)," *Critical Inquiry* 7, no. 1 (October 1, 1980): 121–40, 140.

22 J. K. Rowling, *Harry Potter and the Prisoner of Azkaban* (New York: Scholastic Paperbacks, 2001), 74.

23 Jessica Derschowitz, "J. K. Rowling Responds to Black Hermione Casting for *Harry Potter and the Cursed Child*," *Entertainment Weekly*, December 21, 2015.

24 Leitch, "Twelve Fallacies," 150–53.

25 This approach to film form and technology is often termed "historical poetics"; see David Bordwell, *Poetics of Cinema* (New York: Routledge, 2007) for an influential account.

26 Richard Corliss, *Talking Pictures: Screenwriters in the American Cinema* (New York: Penguin Books, 1975).

27 See Doreen Alexander Child, *Charlie Kaufman: Confessions of an Original Mind* (Santa Barbara: ABC-CLIO, 2010); Derek Hill, *Charlie Kaufman and Hollywood's Merry Band of Pranksters, Fabulists and Dreamers* (New York: Oldcastle Books, 2010) and David LaRocca, *The Philosophy of Charlie Kaufman* (University Press of Kentucky, 2011).

28 For such an approach, see Mario Falsetto, *Stanley Kubrick: A Narrative and Stylistic Analysis*, 2nd edition (Westport, CT: Praeger, 2001).

29 See David Bordwell, *Christopher Nolan: A Labyrinth of Linkages*, 2013, http://www.davidbordwell.net/books/nolan.php.

30 Michel Foucault, "What is an Author?," in *The Foucault Reader* (New York: Pantheon Books, 1984).

31 David Bordwell, *Narration in the Fiction Film* (Madison: University of Wisconsin Press, 1985), 62.

32 Seymour Chatman, *Coming to Terms: The Rhetoric of Narrative in Fiction and Film* (Ithaca, NY: Cornell University Press, 1990).

33 See Bordwell, *Narration in the Fiction Film*.

34 Thanks to Will Hardy and Mai Nardone for their help composing this Thai sentence, which translates to "Without context, it would be nearly impossible to even identify the word 'adaptation' in this sentence."

35 Murray Smith, *Engaging Characters: Fiction, Emotion, and the Cinema* (New York: Oxford University Press, 1995).

36 Noël Carroll, "Toward a Theory of Film Suspense," in *Theorizing the Moving Image* (Cambridge: Cambridge University Press, 1996), 94–124.

37 See Jason Mittell, *Complex TV: The Poetics of Contemporary Television Storytelling* (New York: New York University Press, 2015), for more on the operational aesthetic in narrative.

CHAPTER TWO

Narrative theory and *Adaptation.*

It can be hard to know how to approach a film like *Adaptation.* as a film scholar. Do we try to chronicle its production and reception history, placing it into larger contexts of film and culture? Do we interpret what it says about themes like creativity, commerce, passion, and storytelling? Do we hold up a succession of theoretical lenses to explore how it looks through various analytical prisms? There is no singular correct way to open a discussion of a film, especially one as layered and complex as *Adaptation.*, but a typical way to launch a work of criticism is to offer a brief plot summary to remind viewers what the film is about, assuming that anyone reading this chapter has seen the film at least once. But within the context of narrative theory, what do we mean by "a plot summary"?

Typically, such a summary offers an overview of the film's key narrative events, outlining its story. For *Adaptation.*, we might say that the film is about a Hollywood screenwriter, Charlie Kaufman, struggling to write an adaptation of a nonfiction book that does not seem to have a real plot, and his relationship with his twin brother Donald, who proves to be a more productive and commercially successful screenwriter. But *Adaptation.* is also about the story conveyed in the source material: *New Yorker* reporter Susan Orlean discovering and writing about the story of John Laroche, an eccentric horticulturalist arrested for stealing orchids from protected Florida wetlands. However, as both of these plots suggest, *Adaptation.* tells the story of storytelling itself, suggesting that as much as we might expect a summary of its story, we also need a summary of its narrative discourse. The film takes us inside the thoughts of both Charlie Kaufman and Susan Orlean to dramatize how their writing processes make them reflect on their own passions and obsessions, ranging widely across times and settings to explore these themes with great reflexivity and structural complexity. Additionally and importantly, the film's final act seems quite inconsistent with its first seventy-five minutes in terms of both story and discourse, becoming far more conventional and almost clichéd in its storytelling, suggesting that it either fails as a film or requires some critical reflection to make sense of its narrative choices. Clearly a "summary" is a difficult place to start with *Adaptation.*

Thus for the purposes of this book, I will take a lesson from the study of narrative comprehension, starting the analysis by walking through the film's opening moments to see how it communicates its own approach to meaning-making. As discussed in the previous chapter, the beginning of a film frequently teaches us how to watch it by establishing its norms, expectations, and modes of engagement. So let's start at the beginning of *Adaptation.* to see what we can learn about the film and its approach to narrative.

Before the beginning: *Adaptation.'s* intertexts

Of course, every film has already started before the movie begins. We rarely start watching a film with no knowledge about it, as we bring preconceptions and assumptions forged by paratexts and related contexts. *Adaptation.* is particularly rich with intertextual links, many of which are made explicit within the film's storytelling and might have been known by its original audience in 2002. The most central intertext is Susan Orlean's 1999 nonfiction book *The Orchid Thief*, from which *Adaptation.* is adapted, and before that Orlean's 1995 *New Yorker* essay "Orchid Fever," which provided the foundation of her book.[1] I will discuss Orlean's writings in much more detail below in terms of its vital function as source material, but they seem less important in setting expectations for most viewers—while the book was certainly a success and *The New Yorker* has broad circulation among an educated readership, it is hard to gauge how much *The Orchid Thief* functioned as a framing intertext for viewers coming to see *Adaptation.* The film was not promoted as connected to *The Orchid Thief*, unlike most adaptations that tout the name recognition of their original sources; given its different name, it seems unlikely that many viewers going to the film would know much about the book that was not highlighted in the trailer or poster. Both given the book's status as meditative nonfiction and its lack of hype, it's doubtful that viewers were particularly motivated to seek out the film version of *The Orchid Thief*, even if they had read the book. Thus it would seem fair to say that Orlean's work is more important to most viewers through its dramatization in the film, rather than establishing expectations before watching *Adaptation.*

The film's poster and trailer highlight a different intertext more centrally: the film *Being John Malkovich* (Spike Jonze, 1999). Most of *Adaptation.*'s posters mention this film, and the trailer includes the caption, "From The Academy Award Nominated Creators of *Being John Malkovich*," clearly calling attention to the previous collaboration between director Spike Jonze and writer Charlie Kaufman as an important intertext. *Malkovich*, released in 1999, was the feature film debut for both Jonze, a prominent music video director, and Kaufman, who had written for a number of television comedies throughout the 1990s. The film was a critical darling, celebrated for its compelling execution of a bizarre and enigmatic premise: a puppeteer discovers a portal into the brain of the award-winning actor John Malkovich. While there are few explicit parallels between *Malkovich* and *Adaptation.* in terms of genre, style, or source material, certainly the earlier film cues viewers to expect that *Adaptation.* will break conventions and seem quite atypical compared to most Hollywood movies—whether a viewer had seen the earlier film, the general awareness about it in 2002 would help cue expectations toward the odd and unconventional. The intertext of *Malkovich* proves to be more directly important within *Adaptation.*'s story as well, as much of the action takes place while *Being John Malkovich* is being filmed, and we see the character of Charlie Kaufman on the film set with cameos from its actors. Thus not only does *Malkovich* help establish viewer expectations as to what type of film they might get with *Adaptation.*, it also serves as an internal reference to understand the film's story and characters.

Although we can never account for the wide range of all possible intertextual connections that viewers might encounter prior to watching a film, it is useful to consider three specific types of paratexts as likely reference points for new viewers: a film's trailer, poster, and DVD cover. As Jonathan Gray has argued, such promotional paratexts are essential entry points for viewers, framing expectations, establishing genres and norms, promoting particular interpretations, and otherwise establishing essential contexts for comprehending a film.[2] Unlike many blockbusters with a complex array of different promotional paratexts, *Adaptation.*'s American release featured just one trailer and a single poster design with only slight variations when adapted for home video release, making it fairly straightforward to consider how most viewers might find their first viewing framed by promotional materials.

The poster and DVD cover both feature an image of an orchid in a broken flower pot laying on its side, with Nicolas Cage's partial face appearing on the pot. Graphically, the image seems to tell us little directly about the film, aside from perhaps that Cage will portray a character who is broken in some way, and that flowers or plants might connect to the narrative or character. The text on the poster foregrounds the talent involved in the film, with the names of three stars,

Nicolas Cage, Meryl Streep, and Chris Cooper, prominently displayed above the film's title, all of which use a font reminiscent of a manual typewriter. The other prominent credits read, "Directed by Spike Jonze" and "Screenplay by Charlie Kaufman and Donald Kaufman," distinguished from the standard list of credits at the poster's bottom that appear on nearly all American film posters. It is not surprising that the actors' names are so prominent, as stars are a major way of promoting a film, and both Cage and Streep were well known at the time as quality actors with major awards and a strong reputation for quality performances (if a bit eclectic, in Cage's case); Cooper was less prominent in 2002, although his star was rising after a prominent role in 1999's award-winning *American Beauty* (Sam Mendes). Having such established actors whose names connote quality and prestige help signal that *Adaptation.* will be a creatively distinct film, rather than more conventional Hollywood fare.

The poster's most unusual feature is how it highlights the director and screenwriters equally—it is incredibly rare to promote screenwriters for a film by name, unless it is an individual writer-director such as David Lynch, or based on the screenwriter's prominent novel, as with John Irving's *The Cider House Rules* (Lasse Hallström, 1999). *Adaptation.*'s promotion is even more unusual, given that Jonze and Charlie Kaufman had each only had one produced film credit by 2002, and Donald Kaufman (for reasons that will be discussed below) had no credits whatsoever. Additionally, it is also odd that neither *The Orchid Thief* nor Susan Orlean were promoted on the poster, as she was certainly a more well-known name than Kaufman. The choice to give prominence to the screenwriters over the source material is a conscious framing that significantly shapes how we regard *Adaptation.*

The trailer is more complicated than the poster, but it also directs our attention in similar directions. It's a fairly conventional trailer for an unconventional film, highlighting its stars and presenting a rapid succession of quick moments of humor and drama, and uses an overused popular song, "Under

Pressure" by Queen and David Bowie, that has nothing to do with the film. One notable exception to its conventionality is that it lacks the voice-over narration typical of trailers, choosing instead to use on-screen text to contextualize the film clips, providing a subtle reinforcement of the importance of the written word in this film about writing. This on-screen text consists of five sets of phrases, connected with ellipses:

> "Charlie Kaufman Writes The Way He Lives . . . With Great Difficulty."
> "His Twin Brother Donald Lives The Way He Writes . . . With Foolish Abandon."
> "Susan Writes About Life. . . But Can't Live It."
> "John's Life Is A Book . . . Waiting To Be Adapted."
> "One Story. . . Four Lives . . . A Million Ways It Can End."

What is most significant about these statements is how they focus viewer attention onto the four characters more than any clear narrative events or plot, highlighting three of their roles as writers seemingly working to adapt John's life. The trailer clearly signals that the film will be focused on the process of writing and adapting a book to film, a subject that seems far from compelling for a movie with major Hollywood stars—in fact a notable moment in the trailer is when Cage exclaims the line, "The book has no story!"

One of the goals of a trailer is to provide an advance framework for understanding the film; for *Adaptation.*, the trailer emphasizes characters over plot, and writing over dramatic action, helping to direct our attention and manage our expectations for what the experience of watching the film might be. The trailer sets our expectations in another important way, by shifting its approach significantly around ⅔ through its short running time. Charlie despairingly says the line, "I've written myself into my screenplay," to which Donald responds, "That's kind of weird." The trailer's tone shifts at that moment, as Charlie's dialogue emphasizes all of the "Hollywood things" that he doesn't want to include, like drugs, sex, and car chases, while the quick succession of images portray those very elements as they appear in *Adaptation*. By highlighting these elements, most of which come from *Adaptation.*'s final act, the trailer prepares us for the film's highly reflexive tone and mirrors its final shift from an unconventional meditation on passion and writing, to an action-driven tale of obsession, romance, and self-discovery. Thus while the trailer feels far more conventional than the film it is promoting, in many ways it sets the stage quite effectively for the unique narrative experience of watching *Adaptation*.

Teaching us how to watch *Adaptation*.

We cannot predict what variety of intertexts and contextual knowledge any viewer might bring to a film, but for the purposes of narrative analysis, we can assume that a viewer starts watching a movie from the beginning. The opening scenes of a film work to orient viewers in their comprehension process, situate the film's genre and relevant reference points, establish the main characters, and signal its intrinsic storytelling norms. The first fourteen minutes of *Adaptation.* accomplish many of these goals, and provide a vital roadmap for the entire film.

After the opening logo of Columbia Pictures, a voice emerges over a black screen:

> Do I have an original thought in my head? My bald head? Maybe if I were happier, my hair wouldn't be falling out. Life is short. I need to make the most of it. Today is the first day of the rest of my life. . . . I'm a walking cliché. I really need to go to the doctor and have my leg checked. There's something wrong. A bump. The dentist called again. I'm way overdue.[3]

This monologue continues in a similar vein for a full ninety-eight seconds, over a black screen as the film's credits roll subtly in a small white font at the bottom of the frame. The deadpan voice, which many viewers would certainly recognize as belonging to Nicolas Cage, continues to offer a stream of consciousness litany of self-loathing gripes and worries, with occasional attempts to think positively ("I need to read more, improve myself. What if I learned Russian or something?") and make excuses for what seems to be depression ("Maybe it's my brain chemistry"). What's notable is how little information this opening monologue actually provides to novice viewers: we get none of the typical expository indications about who the character is, what he is doing (aside from being a screenwriter), what situation he is in, or how this might incite a plot for a Hollywood film. After this opening segment, we know almost nothing about the film, what it is about, or even who this person is beyond his own self-loathing. Instead we are left asking questions about both what we have just heard and what it foretells for the film we have just started viewing.

Such a digressive, uninformative, and low-energy opening monologue over a black screen is not how films are supposed to open. Looking at practical theory highlights how unconventional and downright wrong this choice is—Blake Snyder sums up the conventional importance of such openings by writing, "The very first impression of what a movie is—its tone, its mood, the type and scope of the film—are all found in the opening image."[4] Based on these criteria, *Adaptation.*'s opening image is a complete failure, telling us nothing about the narrative scope of the film, and setting a tone and mood that hardly makes viewers want to keep watching. But the opening does tell us quite a bit about the film's approach to storytelling itself. It highlights that *Adaptation.* is willing to aggressively break convention and risk alienating viewers. It alerts us that the film will embrace subjectivity and reflexivity through the intrinsic norm of voice-over narration. And it reveals that even though it will present the subjective perspective of the protagonist (who is soon revealed to be the film's writer himself), it will not take that perspective too seriously, as the tone of Cage's performance and the monologue's hyperdigressive writing style call attention to how ridiculous the character's neurotic perspective truly is. Additionally, the one truly essential bit of story information that is revealed during this sequence is buried within the roll of the credits: the screenplay for the film we are watching was written by both Charlie and Donald Kaufman, a crucial fact whose importance will only be revealed nearly two hours later. Thus while this opening tells us little about story, it reveals more about narrative discourse and tone; suggesting that the relationship between story and discourse will be important for understanding *Adaptation.*

The black screen disappears abruptly, replaced by another unconventional sequence: shaky low-quality video footage pans across a film set, as a voice cuts through the murmur by loudly commanding, "Shut up!" twice, a juxtaposition that might be seen as a direct response to the opening monologue. An on-screen caption situates us as, "On the set of '*Being John Malkovich*,' Summer 1998," establishing this intertextual relationship that the poster and trailer had already emphasized. A further caption reveals that the speaker is "John Malkovich, Actor," as he is instructing his fellow actors how to play the scene. The behind-the-scenes footage continues to reveal other hard-working crew members via captions, including "Thomas Smith, First Assistant Director," and "Lance Acord, Cinematographer" (both of whom play themselves and serve the same roles in the production of *Adaptation.* itself). The footage then cuts to a character played by Nicolas Cage awkwardly standing in the wings observing the action, captioned as "Charlie Kaufman, Screenwriter." The offscreen voice of Thomas Smith addresses him: "You, you're in the eyeline. Can you please get off the stage?" which Charlie obeys by awkwardly walking out the stage door. The next shot cuts to outside the set as Charlie exits the door, with a notable transition from handheld low-quality video to a stable and well-composed film image that typifies the rest of the movie; as Charlie ambles away from the door, his voice-over narration shares his thoughts: "What am I doing here? Why did I bother to come here today? Nobody even seemed to know my name. I've been on this planet for 40 years and I'm no closer to understanding a single thing. Why am I here? How did I get here?"

Even though Charlie's voice-over poses many new questions, this sequence actually does provide some key answers. In terms of story information, we learn that our narrating protagonist is Charlie Kaufman, the screenwriter of *Being John Malkovich* and cowriter of *Adaptation.* itself.[5] This is a huge revelation, as it locates *Adaptation.* within a very small category of films where its screenwriter is an explicit on-screen character (rather than a veiled stand-in for the creator). There are similar films that are adaptations of published memoirs or autobiographies, such as *Eat Pray Love* (Ryan Murphy, 2010) or *American Sniper* (Clint Eastwood, 2014), where the book's author is the main character but it has been adapted by other screenwriters, a function somewhat similar to Susan Orlean in *Adaptation.* There are some memoirs written directly for the screen, such as *Antwone Fisher* (Denzel Washington, 2002) or *A Guide to Recognizing Your Saints* (Dito Montiel, 2006), where an actor plays the screenwriter at an earlier part in his life. Other more experimental films incorporate the writing process into such dramatizations, such as *Naked Lunch* (David Cronenberg, 1991), which fictionalizes the writing of the novel upon which it is based, or *Fear and Loathing in Las Vegas* (Terry Gilliam, 1998), which extends the hallucinatory first-person journalism of Hunter S. Thompson into the realm of the impossible. Films like *Adaptation.*, where the screenwriter character is portrayed at the same point in their lives as they wrote this screenplay, are highly unconventional and rare—*My Dinner with Andre* (Louis Malle, 1981) dramatizes a conversation between two men who play versions of themselves, with Andre Gregory and Wallace Shawn serving as both screenwriters and performers. Some films embrace high levels of reflexivity by making the screenwriter a character and highlighting the process of filmmaking itself, as with *New Nightmare* (Wes Craven, 1994), *The League of Gentlemen's Apocalypse* (Steve Bendelack,

2005), and *This is the End* (Evan Goldberg and Seth Rogen, 2013). All of these examples suggest that by Charlie Kaufman serving as both protagonist and screenwriter, *Adaptation.* is connected to both the realm of nonfiction and highly reflexive approaches to filmmaking. This sequence draws both of these connections: introducing Charlie through pseudo-documentary footage with real people playing themselves situates it within the realm of nonfiction, while commencing the narrative on a film set highlights its reflexive approach.

In terms of storytelling strategies, this segment confirms that voice-over narration will be an ongoing intrinsic norm, offering us deep access to Charlie's thoughts and suggesting that the film's narrative will be highly aligned with this character. Because Charlie's voice-over is so self-deprecating and seemingly honest, we can assume it is both reliable (at least toward what he thinks and feels, if not how others perceive him) and communicative—he seems not to hold back from us viewers, and thus this reinforces our tight alignment to Charlie after only three minutes of the film. Additionally, the use of on-screen captions to identify the place and people suggests that the film itself will use reflexive devices to communicate information, rather than adhering to norms of realism that typify much conventional cinema. The mixture of the opening black screen, the handheld pseudo-documentary footage, and conventional filmmaking all suggest that *Adaptation.* will violate conventions and make unusual stylistic and storytelling choices to convey its ideas and narrative.

This willingness to break convention becomes even clearer in the next segment, as the film answers Charlie's question, "How did I get here?" in a most unusual fashion: cutting to a shot of molten lava, with a caption reading, "Hollywood, CA, Four Billion And Forty Years Earlier." The images begin to speed through a synopsis of evolution over the next minute, from single-cell organisms to plants to dinosaurs to mammals to a final shot of a baby being born, concluding with a close-up of Charlie sitting in a restaurant. This flashback sequence does little to advance the narrative, as Charlie's evolutionary backstory is not particularly useful information, but it reinforces the film's unconventional storytelling strategies, employing footage more suited to a nature documentary to suggest that it will embrace any style or tone to serve the purpose of a joke. Beyond just a joke, however, the evolution sequence introduces a larger thread of dramatizing natural history that will recur throughout the film to illustrate sequences from Orlean's book—later in the film, we see Charlie brainstorm this sequence with the intent to "tie all of history together" on-screen (41). Additionally, the sequence portrays Charlie's inability to think beyond himself, neurotically imagining that all of Earth's evolutionary history has culminated in his own self-loathing. Thus even an unconventional flashback sequence that plays as a joke still reinforces *Adaptation.*'s themes and character elements.

Four minutes into the film, and we have yet to see anything resembling conventional film storytelling—the closest we have got to a narrative event is Charlie being asked to leave the set of *Being John Malkovich*, although that moment functions more as character development than progressing the story. The next scene in the restaurant is both the film's most conventional sequence thus far, and it's most important for the story, functioning as what practical screenwriting theory terms the "inciting incident." However, as inciting incidents go, it is far from dramatic: Charlie discusses possibly writing a screenplay adaptation of *The Orchid Thief* with a Hollywood executive, Valerie (played by Tilda Swinton). Like the moments that precede it, this scene also emphasizes character over plot, starting with Charlie's voice-over lamentation over how much he is sweating. Valerie breaks through his voice-over by saying, "We think you're great" (4). Such an affirmation counters our immersion in Charlie's self-loathing thoughts, suggesting that his imagination of his own image and worth differs greatly from how other characters see him. This is the first of many moments that raise the possibility that Charlie is an unreliable narrator, filtering our experience through his own tortured artistry and insecurities, rather than presenting an objective take on the events. Although his narration is not framed as a deceptive trick, we learn to distrust Charlie's sense of himself and remember that his subjectivity might suffer from self-deception.

Once Valerie interrupts the narration, the rest of the scene plays out quite conventionally, presented as a typical shot/reverse-shot dialogue sequence; however, the content of the dialogue is quite important for establishing the film's relationship between story and discourse. In a discussion of how he might adapt the book, Charlie highlights his appreciation of the book as, "great sprawling *New Yorker* stuff, and I'd want to remain true to that. . . . I'd want to let the movie exist, rather than be artificially plot driven" (5). Valerie responds that she is "not exactly sure what that means," but attentive viewers do: it is like the first few minutes of *Adaptation.*, where introducing character subjectivity and allowing for sprawling digressions into natural history trumps any desire for efficient storytelling with a clear chain of narrative events. Coupled with the opening credit that the film is "Based on the book *The Orchid Thief* by Susan Orlean," this scene suggests the highly unusual possibility that *Adaptation.* will simultaneously function as

FIGURE 2.1 *Charlie Kaufman (Nicolas Cage) sweats profusely as he meets with Valerie to discuss his adaptation of* The Orchid Thief.

an adaptation of Orlean's book and dramatize the process of that adaptation itself. Thus we are taught to regard all of the discussions about cinematic storytelling and screenwriting as potential commentary on the film we are watching, deepening the role of reflexivity as a crucial intrinsic norm.

As Charlie and Valerie further discuss the potential adaptation, they outline two crucial poles of film storytelling that structure our comprehension of *Adaptation.* Charlie indignantly asserts his vision of creating "a movie about flowers" that rejects a host of Hollywood conventions:

> I just don't want to ruin it by making it a Hollywood thing. You know? Like an orchid heist movie or something, or, changing the orchids into poppies and turn it into a movie about drug running, you know? . . . I don't want to cram in sex or guns or car chases. You know? Or characters learning profound life lessons. Or growing, or coming to like each other, or overcoming obstacles to succeed in the end. I mean, the book isn't like that, and life isn't like that. It just isn't. I feel very strongly about this. (5–6)

Charlie's passionate list of things to avoid seemingly runs counter to Valerie's brief mentions of what she values about the book—"Laroche is a fun character, isn't he?"—and how she imagines the film's plot might be changed—"I guess we thought that maybe Susan Orlean and Laroche could fall in love" (5). Thus these dual poles, between "a Hollywood thing," emphasizing fun characters and imposed romance plots, and "sprawling *New Yorker* stuff" about flowers and real life, define Charlie's goal as *Adaptation.*'s protagonist, setting the plot in motion as he seeks to adapt *The Orchid Thief* in a way true to his vision and resisting the pull of mainstream convention. Additionally, this dichotomy structures our understanding of *Adaptation.*'s storytelling itself, as we recognize that the film we are watching will also be straddling these dual coasts of Hollywood formula and New York intellectualism.

The next scene introduces a new set of conventions and characters that prove vital to *Adaptation.*'s storytelling strategies. Cutting to an establishing shot of a New York skyscraper, with the caption, "*New Yorker* Magazine, Three Years Earlier," the film opts for an East Coast sensibility, at least for the moment. We hear a voice-over narration spoken by Meryl Streep: "John Laroche is a tall guy, skinny as a stick, pale-eyed, slouch-shouldered, and sharply handsome, in spite of the fact that he is missing all his front teeth" (6). This line is also the opening sentence of both Susan Orlean's 1995 *New Yorker* story and *The Orchid Thief*, offering a strong contrast in tone and timbre from Charlie's previous narration: while Charlie speaks only about himself in self-deprecating terms, Susan provides vivid descriptions of somebody else, making the narration more broad and inclusive. Films rarely include multiple voice-over narrators, but *Adaptation.* justifies this norm visually by cutting to images of Streep as Orlean typing in her office surrounded by research materials on orchids, suggesting that we are hearing her writing her book, a common convention for conveying the written word on film. Susan continues in voice-over to convey that two years earlier, she went to Florida to report on a story about an orchid theft from a state preserve, introducing Laroche's story that she recounts in both her article and book. This brief sequence follows from the previous scene by establishing some of the ways that *Adaptation.* will function as an adaptation of *The Orchid Thief*: it will include Orlean's direct language via voice-over, and portray Orlean herself as a character writing her book, seemingly paralleling Charlie's own writing process. Six minutes into the film and we have established two main characters with parallel goals: writing their accounts of John Laroche in two different media.

As Susan's voice-over finishes, we cut to a new outdoors scene with another caption, "State Road 29, Florida, Two Years Earlier." We see a white van turn off the road, cutting into the van's interior to reveal a mess of garbage and gardening junk while the driver listens to the audio book version of *The*

Writings of Charles Darwin discussing natural selection. This scene lasts for three and a half minutes, following numerous cinematic conventions for the first time: no voice-over, frequent ellipses to compress hours of action into a minute of screen time, and the presence of a background musical score to heighten the mood. The action of the scene directly dramatizes what Susan's voice-over described: "A white man and three Seminole men [were] arrested with rare orchids they'd stolen out of a place called the Fakahatchee Strand State Preserve" (6). The scene introduces Chris Cooper's John Laroche as a main character, and sets in motion the legal storyline concerning his use of Seminoles as a legal cover to enable him to steal protected plants. This scene demonstrates one way that *Adaptation.* will adapt Orlean's book: direct dramatization of the events she describes via conventional narrative filmmaking. If the film were a more conventional adaptation, this might well be the opening scene, putting the plot into motion via the inciting incident of Laroche's theft and arrest; in fact, such a possibility is explored a few minutes later in the film, as we see Charlie writing the first words of his script (and hear him narrating them): "We open on State Road 29. A battered white van speeds along making a sharp skidding right into the Fakahatchee Strand State Preserve. The driver of the van is a skinny man with no front teeth. This is John Laroche" (17). Instead of following this conventional dramatic opening, Charlie eventually revises his approach to a more radically reflexive mode; after such revisions, these sequences function as an embedded storytelling frame, dramatizing Susan's accounts of Laroche within the film's portrayal of her writing process.

This scene creates some temporal complexity by adding a third storyline in a third timeline: the real Laroche was arrested on December 21, 1993, with Orlean arriving to report on the case days later. Susan writing her book in New York presumably starts in late 1995, as the *New Yorker* article was published in January 1995 and her book was originally published in January 1999. Charlie's process of adaptation starts in summer of 1998, per the earlier caption, although this requires some dramatic license since *The Orchid Thief* would not have been released yet—the actual Kaufman began adapting the book based on prepublication galleys, while the fictional Charlie references a published hardcover copy throughout the film. *Adaptation.* uses captions to keep us temporally oriented, using relational phrasings like "Two Years Earlier" to help viewers track the chronology. This intrinsic norm suggests that even within such a complex and nonobvious film, some narrative elements must be presented as clearly as possible to maximize comprehension, as the filmmakers prioritize which facets should maximize clarity and which should allow for ambiguity.

The next scene cuts to Charlie entering the front door of his home, without any caption to reorient us in time and place—since captions have already established the three threads of Florida in 1993, New York in 1995, and Hollywood in 1998 (as well as four billion and forty years earlier), the film asks viewers to remember these separate story threads, using captions only occasionally as a reminder or to introduce new historical moments. As Charlie enters, an offscreen voice calls out, "Charles, is that you?" A perceptive viewer will recognize that voice as Nicolas Cage, creating a moment of confusing character recognition: why is Charlie's voice offscreen while we see him on-screen? We get our answer as Charlie climbs the stairs to reveal another character played by Cage lying on the floor in the hallway. As their dialogue proceeds for the next two minutes, we learn that this is Donald Kaufman, and he is staying with his brother while unemployed. Donald reveals that he wants to be a screenwriter as well, and he plans to take a screenwriting seminar from Robert McKee. Charlie argues with Donald's Hollywood-centered approach to screenwriting ("Donald, don't say 'industry'"), and contends that "screenwriting seminars are bullshit" (10), prompting a debate over whether films should follow principles, even when they are about flowers; as Charlie says, "Nobody's ever done a movie about flowers before. So there are no guidelines" (11). Their conversation revisits the two poles established in the restaurant scene, with Donald representing Hollywood conventions while Charlie struggles to break new ground: "Writing is a journey into the unknown. It's not building one of your model airplanes!" (12), contrasting the act of artistic exploration with a craft approach to story construction.

This scene is crucial to both the thematic considerations of art versus craft, and the film's approach to character. In introducing *Adaptation.*'s fourth main character, the film must grapple with the challenge of recognizing the difference between two characters played by the same actor, an issue that does not matter for written narratives that can easily just signal character names. Much of this differentiation stems from Cage's performance, giving Donald a much more energetic and upbeat demeanor to contrast with Charlie's slouching physicality and droopy voice. Costuming is also key, establishing a pattern where Charlie nearly always wears a schlumpy outfit of an unbuttoned plaid flannel shirt over a plain T-shirt, while Donald wears more put-together button-down shirts or sweaters. Most importantly going forward, the film never attempts to confuse viewers about which brother is on-screen, as other characters can easily distinguish between them, with dialogue and contexts always orienting us to recognize the correct character. Like with its orienting captions, *Adaptation.* avoids creating unnecessary confusion by relying upon convention and clarity except for when ambiguity is actually the goal. Instead, the pairing of Charlie and Donald works via contrast rather than confusion, presenting them with the parallel goals of writing a screenplay but dramatizing drastically different approaches and outcomes in their storylines.

In introducing Donald, the film reveals its first major fictional character, although it makes no overt acknowledgment of the difference between characters based on real people (Charlie, Susan, John), and those who were created for the film (Donald, Valerie). In fact, the earliest mention of Donald suggests that he is a real person: the opening credits notably read, "Screenplay by Charlie Kaufman and Donald Kaufman," a claim that, as discussed later, is essential for understanding the entire film. A first-time viewer would have little reason to doubt Donald's status as real, as credited screenwriters must be real people—Kaufman had to specially petition the Writer's Guild to allow Donald to be given credit. Thus in its function as a nonfiction adaptation, *Adaptation.* generally presents itself as a true story, leading viewers to assume that new characters are based on real people. This scene also indirectly introduces two new characters who will appear later: screenwriting guru Robert McKee, as referenced by Donald's dialogue, and violinist Amelia Kavan, whose picture from a newspaper cutout Charlie longingly admires while lying in bed. Again, there are no markers to suggest that McKee is based on a real person and Amelia is a character wholly invented for the film, continuing the default assumption that *Adaptation.* is presenting a dramatic version of real people and events, rather than a fictionalization.

The next scene concludes what I would call the film's opening section by introducing one last important storyline. Charlie sits on a floor with Amelia (played by Cara Seymour), awkwardly withdrawn from the social action of a party; we hear Charlie's voice-over again, obsessing over how to behave with her. The resulting dialogue reveals that they have been friends for eight months, that Amelia regards him as a problem to be solved ("We're gonna solve the whole Charlie Kaufman mess once and for all"), and that she views his acceptance of "the orchid script" as a step forward: "I think it will be good for you to get out of your head. I think it'll ground you to think about the bigger picture, about nature and stuff" (13). While nothing is overtly spoken, it is clearly implied that Charlie and Amelia have the potential for a romantic relationship, if only he would initiate things. The scene establishes an additional goal for Charlie, creating parallel romantic and professional plots for the protagonist that are quite common for Hollywood films; Amelia's attention to Charlie's career links the two goals, suggesting if he succeeds in writing the script, he might win her love. This parallelism is reinforced by having both Amelia and Valerie played by British actresses of comparable age and appearance, highlighting how each goal strives to please one of a pair of similar women.

By the film's fourteen-minute mark, we have learned a great deal about both *Adaptation.*'s story and its storytelling, teaching us how to watch the film going forward. The film's protagonist Charlie has two central goals—writing and romance—with two secondary characters paired to each goal. The film's two other writers, Susan and Donald, also are portrayed as striving to write their respective projects, each with contrasting approaches to Charlie. John Laroche is introduced as the subject of Susan and Charlie's writing, not as a character with his own overt goals—the film's plot is not about Laroche's trial and crime, but rather about how two writers try to capture and dramatize those events. The film is framed as both nonfiction, portraying real people and events, and reflexive metafiction, portraying and reflecting on the act of its own creation. Its approach to storytelling is introduced as at once experimental and unconventional, using highly subjective narration, embedded story layers, and digressive flashbacks, and traditional in its efforts to orient viewers via temporal captions and clearly differentiated characters. The thematic contrast between writing as creative original exploration and expertly crafted entertainment is embodied in the film's style itself, as it offers both experimentation and convention within its opening minutes, alerting viewers to pay close attention to how *Adaptation.* tells its story as a clue to understand it.

Dramatizing practical theory in an impractical film

In this book's introduction, I noted that *Adaptation.* is the rare film where theory is needed to make sense of its own narrative. While the film's opening provides us with many lessons toward making sense of what is to follow, as the film progresses, it is useful to bring in outside resources to strengthen and deepen our understanding. Thus instead of proceeding with the slow-motion walkthrough of the film started above, I will open up our toolbox of narrative theory to see what concepts and approaches can help shine a light on *Adaptation.*, especially as the film's reflexivity and construction become more complex. At the fourteen-minute mark, the film has already called overt attention to one narrative theorist through the highly unusual act of citation through film dialogue: Robert McKee.

Donald's embrace of McKee as a guiding figure highlights much of what practical theory has to offer our understanding of the film, providing a commentary on the dramatized screenwriting practices of both Kaufman brothers. In his first scene, Donald frames McKee's advice as principles rather than rules: "McKee writes that a rule says you must do it this way. A principle says this works and has through all remembered time" (11). Thus in all that follows, we are asked to treat McKee's ideas as effective conventions that work, rather than rigid rules to obey—the fact that *Adaptation.* disobeys nearly all of McKee's principles is not to be held against it, but rather highlights how the film functions as an experiment in breaking convention without refuting the value and usefulness of such conventions. In his book *Story*, McKee describes the Antiplot, an uncommon approach to storytelling that effectively characterizes *Adaptation.*: "This set of anti structure variations doesn't reduce the Classical but reverses it, contradicting traditional forms to exploit, perhaps ridicule the very idea of formal principles. The Antiplot-maker is rarely interested in understatement or quiet austerity; rather, to make clear his 'revolutionary' ambitions, his films tend toward extravagance and self-conscious overstatement."[6] Thus *Adaptation.* is not ultimately a wholesale rebuke of Hollywood conventions or even practical theory like McKee's; instead, it audaciously offers another model to demonstrate how conventions can be productively and entertainingly broken.

The next time McKee is invoked is in a short sequence where Donald is reading his book while Charlie is pouring over *The Orchid Thief.* While the dialogue does not reference McKee, Donald does discuss how he pitched his screenplay to their mother, who "said it was *Silence of the Lambs* meets *Psycho*" (21), a line that plays as a joke to mock Charlie's hyper-commercial derivative approach. However, it emphasizes a key insight of practical theory: all stories are built upon previous examples, and successful storytellers learn what worked for influential predecessors. Even though Charlie touts his own originality, scenes of him pouring over *The Orchid Thief* highlight how his own work is indebted to other writers, as is true of all adaptations. One key premise of McKee and other practical theorists is that creating original narratives requires a clear understanding of the underlying design principles that pervade most previous works, so we should study how they are structured to learn from earlier successes—something Charlie is reluctant to do for his script which he claims has no precedents.

The next citation of McKee comes as Charlie is struggling to make progress with his script, as Donald bursts in buzzing from McKee's seminar and touting his genius. Donald describes one of McKee's lessons to his brother: "He's all for originality, just like you. But he says we have to realize that we all write in a genre, and we must find our originality within that genre. . . . My genre's thriller. What's yours?" (42). Connecting to the previous discussion of Donald's influences, this reference to McKee challenges Charlie's assertions that his work is purely original and affirms the role of genre norms and conventions. Donald's question never is fully answered, however, and it is unclear exactly what genre *Adaptation.* might fall into. In McKee's book, it would probably fit with the last of his list of twenty-five genres, Art Film, following the Antiplot model "with its own complex of formal conventions of structure and cosmology," countering Charlie's own pride of originality and assertions that he is breaking new ground.[7] And yet there is little doubt that the particular combination of norms, influences, and techniques that *Adaptation.* mixes is unique, lacking clear precedents for portraying a screenwriter writing the film we are watching, for blurring a nonfiction story with highly fictionalized elements, and for reflexively calling attention to the practical theory undergirding the very filmmaking practices we are watching.

Donald's next celebratory reference to McKee touts his concept of an Image System, which he claims "greatly increases the complexity of an aesthetic emotion" (51). In *Story*, McKee elaborates on this concept, defining Image Systems as patterns of imagery that reinforce themes and meanings but "must be handled with virtual invisibility and go consciously unrecognized."[8] While imagery and symbolism in *Adaptation.* are not overt, they are also not quite invisible, with at least two motifs in play throughout the film. The first are flowers, which is the purported topic of *The Orchid Thief*, and Charlie's stated goal is to make a film about flowers. Within the film, flowers are often visualized during the dramatization of Laroche's story, as well as illustrating some of the natural history lessons drawn from Orlean's book. Charlie draws connections between flowers and women, co-opting Susan's voice-over categorizing orchid species to his own narration categorizing women he sees. Throughout the film, flowers are symbolically linked with objects of desire, whether literally as John's goal to procure a ghost orchid, associatively resonant with Charlie's unfulfilled sexual desire for multiple women, or thematically connected to Susan's own desire "to know what it feels like to care about something passionately" (26). In these instances, *Adaptation.* uses flowers as a stand-in for passion, making them simultaneously the subject of the film and an object of desire.

The film's second Image System builds upon the double meaning of the film's title, linking adaptation to its role in evolution, where survival is limited to those who can adapt to changing environments. Charlie articulates this symbolic linkage via voice-over after we see a historical flashback to Darwin writing his theory: "It is a journey of evolution. Adaptation. The journey we all take. A journey that unites each and every one of us" (40). We can see Charlie's character arc as evolutionary, as he learns to adapt to the hostile habitat of commercial Hollywood and survive by writing a script suitable to be filmed; additionally, he proves to be more adaptable and resilient than his twin brother, surviving while Donald dies, and thus he is able to "reproduce" through the creative means of filmmaking. It is important to note that symbolism and imagery is not typically the domain of narrative theory; as discussed in the Introduction, narrative critics focus more on analyzing formal elements of storytelling rather than interpreting subtext and themes. However, practical theory can include more than just narrative form, as McKee's advice includes such attention to underlying meanings as well as the mechanics of storytelling.

Returning to the film's overt references to McKee, Donald follows his discussion of imagery by posting a copy of McKee's Ten Commandments next to Charlie's desk. We can only see these commandments briefly, but they contain advice that actually adheres mostly to what Charlie has been arguing: respect your audience, do research, avoid cheap surprises or unearned complications, dramatize exposition, and consider subtext. The film doesn't dwell on these, as Donald proceeds to tell Charlie that he is mixing genres in his script *The Three* by adding an upbeat pop song, "Happy Together," to his thriller, which McKee endorses via the precedent of *Casablanca* (Michael Curtiz, 1942). This call for mixed genres both resonates with *Adaptation.*'s own combination of reflexive comedy and intellectual explorations of natural history from Orlean's book, and foreshadows the film's concluding moments where "Happy Together" plays over a time-lapse sequence of flowers blooming. Yet again, McKee's practical theory guides our own understanding of *Adaptation.*'s construction and storytelling strategies.

McKee's culminating appearance represents his ideas beyond citation or dialogue references: around two-thirds into the film, Charlie attends McKee's seminar in New York in a desperate attempt to get a handle on his script. McKee, played by Brian Cox, appears on stage to lecture an adoring crowd on writing screenplays, with Charlie sitting in the audience, watching with skepticism; Charlie's voice-over drowns out McKee's blustery lecture, as he obsesses over his own worthlessness and regrets coming to the seminar. As Charlie rises to leave, McKee cuts through the voice-over with the admonition, "And God help you if you use voice-over in your work, my friends! God help you! It's flaccid, sloppy writing! Any idiot can write voice-over narration to explain the thoughts of a character" (67–68). Charlie seems affected by this comment, and decides to stay through the seminar; *Adaptation.* is also affected by this comment, as Charlie's voice-over ceases for the rest of the film until its very last scene, when his voice-over acknowledges, "McKee would not approve" (99). This moment highlights the film's reflexive use of practical theory, as the principles and guidance offered by McKee helps shape and comment upon the storytelling of *Adaptation.* itself. Of course, the film's dramatization of McKee is not faithful to his written advice, as McKee never bans voice-over as such, but as discussed in the previous chapter, emphasizes that film should dramatize information and emotion rather than telling them via words more suitable for other media.

The direct impact of practical theory upon the film's storytelling is deepened in the subsequent scenes that are crucial to the film's narrative development. McKee pronounces, "You cannot have a protagonist without desire!," counter to Charlie's own sense of his screenplay. Charlie musters the courage to ask McKee a question: "What if a writer is attempting to create a story where nothing much happens? Where people don't change, they don't have any epiphanies. They struggle and are frustrated, and nothing is resolved. More a reflection of the real world." McKee dramatically refutes Charlie on two fronts: first on a practical level, "You write a screenplay without conflict or crisis, you'll bore your audience to tears" (68). On a more philosophical level, McKee lambasts Charlie's perception that nothing much happens in real life, indignantly reeling off a litany of realistic events and decisions that happen everyday which incorporate high-stakes drama. Charlie seems moved by this, approaching him after the lecture for more advice: "What you said this morning shook me to the bone. What you said was bigger than my screenwriting choices. It was about my choices as a human being" (69–70). In this sequence, we see practical theory dramatized and functioning as a crucial moment of character transformation, drastically challenging Charlie's sense of self, both as a writer and a person. And given the metafictional way that *Adaptation.* allows Charlie's on-screen actions to affect the film itself, McKee's power impacts the film's storytelling as well.

McKee's final appearance follows this encounter, as Charlie buys him a drink for some personal advice on his screenplay. Charlie charts his approach to *The Orchid Thief*: "I wanted to present it simply, without big character arcs or sensationalizing the story. I wanted to show flowers as God's miracles. I wanted to show that Orlean never saw the blooming ghost orchid. It was about disappointment." McKee quickly rejects the premise: "That's not a movie. You gotta go back, put in the drama" (70). The debate that emerged in the film's early scenes reoccurs here, with Charlie trying to stick with his vision of creating a meandering film about flowers true to Orlean's book, while Valerie, Donald, and his agent encouraged him to find a genre, add romance, and "make up a crazy story" (51) to follow conventional filmmaking. McKee provides a crucial way out of his dilemma:

> I'll tell you a secret. The last act makes the film. Wow them in the end and you got a hit. You can have flaws, problems, but wow them in the end and you've got a hit. Find an ending. But don't cheat. And don't you dare bring in a *deus ex machina*. Your characters must change. And the change must come from them. Do that and you'll be fine. (70)

McKee's advice becomes a road map for *Adaptation.*'s final act, where a dramatic shift in both storytelling style and story

FIGURE 2.2 *Charlie Kaufman (Nicolas Cage) meets with Robert McKee (Brian Cox), who guides him toward a powerful ending.*

content aims to "wow them in the end" and solve Charlie's adaptation problems.

McKee's final lines offer a clue as to how Charlie might "find an ending" without cheating. McKee asks Charlie if he's taken his seminar before, and Charlie explains that it was his twin brother Donald. Marveling at twin screenwriters, McKee notes that the "finest screenplay ever written," *Casablanca*, was written by twins, Julius and Philip Epstein (71). This connects to the film's next scene, as Charlie calls Donald to invite him to come to New York to offer some feedback on his script. This moment is the crucial turning point triggering the film's climactic and confounding final act, as discussed more below; notably it is the direct by-product of advice from the film's embodiment of practical theory, Robert McKee. Thus *Adaptation.* features the highly unusual device of putting a theorist and his well-known book of practical theory as dramatized aspects of the fictional film, inviting viewers to pay close attention to his theoretical concepts and consider how they might guide our understanding of the film we are watching both playing out on-screen and being written within the story itself.

Analyzing *Adaptation.*'s structure with practical theory

As discussed in the Introduction, practical theory is typically used to guide the creation of new work, while critical theory seeks to analyze and understand works that have already been made. Yet we can also use practical theory as an analytic lens, exploring how a film meets or deviates from those practical norms and guidelines. Clearly *Adaptation.* invites such connections through its dramatization of McKee and his approach to screenwriting, but we can go beyond what the film portrays and consider broader practical concepts around film storytelling as part of our toolbox for narrative analysis.

The act structure of films is both the most commonly discussed aspect of practical film theory and the most essential concept for understanding *Adaptation.* While McKee is more flexible than most screenwriting theorists about the necessity of a three-act structure, he too contends that the majority of films follow that canonical model, with four crucial scenes for the main plot: an Inciting Incident and climactic turning points for each of the three acts.[9] In *Adaptation.*, the low-key-inciting incident for the film's main plot is clear, as Charlie takes the assignment of adapting *The Orchid Thief* for the screen. But importantly, this plot does not follow a typical three-act structure, as it lacks external obstacles, stakes-raising complications, or surprising reversals—instead, Charlie struggles with writer's block with little variation or new roadblocks for the film's first seventy-five minutes. This ambling storytelling is more akin to art cinema as a tradition, keeping with the idea of "a story where nothing much happens" that Charlie asks McKee about, and thus it appears that a conventional act structure does not help us understand the film.

However, an unconventional use of act structure is crucially important to the film. As discussed above, *Adaptation.*'s opening minutes cue us to pay attention to narrative discourse as well as story—it is in the realm of discourse and storytelling that the film adheres to norms of structure, acts, and turning points. If we consider the film's narrative discourse, we can see that the film actually breaks down clearly into four acts, in keeping with Kristin Thompson's argument that typical three-act structures actually contain an important turning point in the middle of the film. As discussed above, *Adaptation.*'s first act establishes an unconventional storytelling mode, with subjective voice-over, historical digressions such as the evolution sequence, and the nested plot of Susan reporting on Laroche's story. The rest of the first act continues along these conventions and focal points, establishing the main characters, their relationships, and a long stretch dramatizing Laroche's story as filtered through Susan's reporting.

At the thirty-minute mark, we get a new storytelling device added to the film's repertoire of techniques: we see a sequence where Charlie attends an orchid show with Alice the waitress that culminates in a romantic encounter, but these moments are revealed to be a masturbatory fantasy as we cut to Charlie in his bedroom. While Charlie's story of writer's block doesn't change significantly at this moment, the film's storytelling does, adding another layer of complication to the narrative mechanisms used to convey its portrayal of "nothing much happening." These complications become quite relevant to viewers, as we are left to wonder throughout the rest of the film whether scenes are "real" within the film's storyworld or Charlie's subjective fantasies. This second act features two other masturbatory fantasies, as Charlie imagines sex with both Valerie and Susan.

Importantly, this narrative technique is introduced when Donald interrupts Charlie's masturbation to describe the concept for his screenplay, *The Three*. Within *Adaptation.*, Donald's script functions as a counterpoint to Charlie's fledging adaptation, hewing to Hollywood conventions, genres, structures, and McKee's various guidelines for successful storytelling. However, it is also completely incoherent: the thriller dramatizes a cop chasing a serial killer who has abducted a female victim, but in the final twist, it's revealed that "the killer really suffers from multiple personality disorder. . . . He's actually really the cop, and the girl, all of them are him!" (30–31). None of the other characters except Charlie see how such a twist is impossible to visualize on-screen without unfairly deceiving the audience, and other characters regard Donald's script as brilliant and complex. One on level, *The Three* works as a satire of hackneyed Hollywood conventions to highlight what *Adaptation.* itself is not; on another, it calls attention to how moments in *Adaptation.* do actually deceive the audience, as with the previous sequence of Charlie's fantasy. However, these two scenes in tandem emphasize that even if *Adaptation.* portrays events on-screen that didn't "really" happen, it will play fair with the audience by grounding our comprehension rather than tricking us.

Adaptation. continues to introduce new narrative norms to keep the storytelling moving forward even as Charlie's story process continues to stagnate. At the forty-minute mark, another minor turning point merges the plot of Charlie's writing process and the film's storytelling techniques—in a moment of inspiration, Charlie dictates a sequence for his script that dramatizes the history of evolution identically to the sequence from the beginning of the film. This moment is too minor to signal a clear act break, but it makes the film's mode of reflexivity concrete: the script that Charlie is writing is the film we are viewing. Again, the introduction of a new narrative element is reinforced by following it with Donald presenting contrasting conventional norms, as he basks in the afterglow of McKee's seminar and relays his thoughts on finding originality within a genre. By highlighting the conventionality of Donald's writing and McKee's guidance, *Adaptation.* reminds us to pay attention to its own unconventional techniques which are to become even more important to understanding the film as it proceeds.

The next and arguably most important development in the film's expansion of its storytelling techniques comes at its midway point—at the fifty-eight-minute mark, Charlie bemoans in voice-over that he cannot connect with Orlean's story: "I have no understanding of anything outside of my own panic and self-loathing and pathetic, little existence. It's like the only thing I'm actually qualified to write about is myself and my own self" (58). Inspiration strikes and he dictates the early restaurant scene where he and Valerie discuss *The Orchid Thief*, describing "Charlie Kaufman, fat, old, bald, repulsive," in a manner evocative of the film's opening voice-over (59). This moment functions as the key turning point between acts, as Charlie officially writes himself and his writing process into the script he is writing. For viewers, this confirms that everything we are watching has been authored by Charlie the character, not just Kaufman the actual screenwriter, creating a highly reflexive experience that requires viewing with a high degree of awareness of its own construction and attention to the operational aesthetic.

As with the other turning points in narrative discourse, this one is also punctuated by Donald—interrupting Charlie's more engaged yet still tortured writing process, Donald announces that he has finished his script of *The Three*. In discussing the script, Donald references the image of a snake eating itself, Ouroboros, which prompts Charlie to highlight his own process: "I'm Ouroboros. . . . I've written myself into my screenplay. . . . It's self-indulgent. It's narcissistic. It's solipsistic. It's pathetic. I'm pathetic" (60). This dialogue calls our attention to this new structural technique, ensuring that viewers understand how Charlie's script is playing out in front of our eyes, while also reinforcing Charlie's own character deficiencies and self-loathing. The scene ends with a dramatic decision that signals the next act: Charlie decides to go to New York to meet Susan, while Donald mentions that he could also go to McKee's seminar being held in New York the next weekend. Thus at the film's midpoint, both the story and storytelling feature turning points that signal new directions.

The film's second half is somewhat out of balance, with a short third act of only fifteen minutes that pulls back from the storytelling experiments of the film's first half. This act uses no fantasy sequences or dramatized historical moments, but rather features dramatized sequences from Orlean's book, as well as scenes of Charlie in New York. Aside from the key scene in McKee's seminar discussed above, voice-over is minimized, leading to a wordless scene of more than a minute in an elevator where Charlie anxiously fails to speak with Susan—the lack of voice-over is noticeable from this sequence, but after an hour living in Charlie's head, viewers can easily imagine his tortured thought process as he tries to say something. The key scenes in this act are Charlie's interactions with McKee discussed above, with voice-over used copiously to convey Charlie's dismay at being at the seminar until McKee chides screenwriters for using that lazy technique, banishing it until the film's final scene. This third act features the film's most naturalistic style of storytelling, portraying the key events of Charlie failing to meet Susan and having an epiphany with McKee in a highly straightforward and non-reflexive mode (aside from the voice-over gag), notably lacking scenes of Charlie actually writing.

The vital transition into the film's final act is inspired by McKee's admonition to "find an ending" and reference to the Epsteins as twin screenwriters: Charlie invites Donald to New York to read his script and asks, "How would the great Donald end this script?" (74). From this moment forward, *Adaptation.* becomes a very different film in terms of both story and storytelling. Stylistically, its storytelling becomes highly conventional, with more use of atmospheric, emotionally cueing music, total lack of subjective fantasies or voice-over, and editing and cinematography typical of Hollywood thrillers, stripping the film of much of its distinctiveness. In terms of story, the film becomes simultaneously more outlandish and conventional, checking off every item on Charlie's initial laundry list of what elements to avoid being "a Hollywood thing": a drug-fueled sexual relationship between Susan and John, guns, car chases, learning life lessons, and "overcoming obstacles to succeed in the end" (6). It also swerves far from the nonfiction source material, as nothing in the final act is either derived from the book or happened in real life; these sensational events are overtly fictionalized, with Laroche killed by an alligator and Susan arrested, which are clearly untrue given both real people's attendance at the film's premiere. At times the final act feels like an extended fantasy sequence, but it lacks any revelation to suggest that it is "unreal" within the film's storyworld. It is fair to say that the final act of *Adaptation.* feels like a completely different film.

The important question is why? Given how much the film cues us to pay attention to its own narrative techniques and explores the reflexive blur between story and storytelling, it seems unlikely that it was simply a case of shoddy filmmaking, even though that might be the first instinct of some viewers and critics. Instead, we need to pay attention to the film's representations of practical theory to understand its major tonal shift. For its first two-thirds, Charlie is a neurotic mess unsure about nearly everything in his life except his artistic beliefs to be original and resist "selling out" to Hollywood conventions, a position articulated in his conversations with Donald. After McKee's seminar, Charlie admits that his advice made him rethink everything, both as a screenwriter and "my choices as a human being" (70). The final act flows from this epiphany, flowing from Charlie's newfound willingness to follow "guidelines" and heed McKee's advice to "wow them in the end." Additionally, it adheres to the boldness that McKee wrote about the Antiplot, with "extravagance and self-conscious overstatement" to reverse and contradict classical principles.[10] But to fully understand how this transition and final act makes sense, both conceptually and thematically, we need to go back into our toolbox to explore three more key concepts: adaptation, character, and authorship.

What kind of adaptation is *Adaptation.*?

Donald, voicing the wisdom of McKee, encourages Charlie to find his genre to guide and structure his writing. Charlie never does seem to find a single genre to ground his writing, and Kaufman does not seem interested in placing *Adaptation.* into a traditional genre either: the film is typically called a comedy, because it is very funny, but it features very few other conventions of comedies in terms of plot, performance style, narrative techniques, or themes. Certainly, Charlie's goal of creating a film that is more original and true to the book's nonnarrative style seems to have made the film atypical for conventional genres, as the characters note that "films about flowers" are far from an established genre. But might we think of the film's genre not in terms of its narrative structure and norms, but rather the cultural category that might be most productive in classifying it? If so, then the film clearly marks its own categorical belongingness in its title: adaptations.

How might concepts explored within adaptation theory help us understand *Adaptation.*? As discussed in Chapter 1, the most frequent concept cited by scholars of adaptation is fidelity, trying to discern how true to the original text an adaptation might be. On first glance, *Adaptation.* is a glaring example of a remarkably unfaithful adaptation of *The Orchid Thief*: it focuses far less on Orlean's reporting of Laroche's story than Kaufman's attempts to adapt the book, adding new characters, events, and settings along the way, and even creating a completely fictionalized and sensational conclusion of a nonfiction book that kills off its subject and places its author in jail! Of course, faithfulness seems like an unfair measure to judge this film that so clearly and overtly highlights its own failures to adapt the book, which in itself might be wholly unadaptable via traditional terms. But rather than dismissing questions of fidelity as wholly irrelevant, we might consider how issues of fidelity and truth matter within the film's metafiction itself.

Charlie regularly mentions how nondramatic *The Orchid Thief* is, and how ill-suited it is to the norms of dramatic filmmaking. Instead, he says that its beauty and power come from Orlean's descriptive musings on orchids and her compelling characterization of Laroche. The film frequently delivers on these two elements through Susan's voice-over narration reading long passages from the book, allowing Orlean's prose to remain central to the experience. As discussed in Chapter 1, voice-over narration is often regarded as a non-cinematic technique, drawn more from literature than film; however, as Sarah Kozloff argues, voice-over in film is cinematic in its use of sound, performance, tone, and timing. Thus having Meryl Streep read passages from Orlean's book in character is not the same as a reader's experience with the book, as her distinctive performance and vocal delivery adds tonal variety and depth to the language. Additionally, since Susan is a character in the film, the use of voice-over does more than just repeat Orlean's prose—it helps develop her fictionalized character.

One of the book's most thematically important passages dramatized within *Adaptation.* comes while Susan is hosting a dinner party at her home, where her sophisticated New York friends and husband are mockingly reacting to her tales of Laroche. She withdraws to the bathroom, with her voice-over revealing her interior thoughts: "I wanted to want something as much as people wanted these plants. But it isn't in my constitution. I suppose I do have one unembarrassed passion: I want to know what it feels like to care about something passionately" (26). This passage is nearly verbatim from Orlean's book, but it is presented within a drastically different context: in the book, it comes after Orlean visits the Fakahatchee Preserve searching for a ghost orchid but coming up short, reflecting on her inability to relate to the obsessions of orchid hunters and thus reinforcing the divide between Orlean's journalistic detachment and the passions of the orchid collectors. By shifting this crucial reflection to her interior monologue reacting to her friends and family, it recontextualizes her sense of disconnection from her home context of New York sophisticates, thus setting the stage for Susan's character arc of fulfilling her desires with Laroche in Florida. Is this a faithful adaptation of the book? On the one hand, it is a word-for-word reproduction of one of the book's central passages that expresses a core idea—in fact, *Adaptation.*

embraces an intrinsic norm that for its first two-thirds, nearly every phrase spoken via Susan's voice-over is a direct quotation from *The Orchid Thief*. But on the other hand, this example transforms its context and thus its thematic meaning and connection to character. Thus the sequence functions simultaneously as a faithful representation of the book and a transformation of its ideas into a new context—a process resonating with the evolutionary concept of "adaptation" that runs throughout the film.

Themes of fidelity and recontextualization pervade *Adaptation.*, as Charlie aims to be true to Orlean's *New Yorker*-style book while adapting it to the hostile environment of Hollywood storytelling. While the film's approach to adaptation is highly idiosyncratic, it does fit with paradigms explored by adaptation theory. In Thomas Leitch's taxonomy of ten different modes of adaptation, he singles out *Adaptation.* as paradigmatic of the category *deconstruction*, which he defines as "films whose subject is the problems involved in producing texts." He writes that "*Adaptation.* achieves its comic effect by showing that anything like a faithful

FIGURE 2.3 *Susan Orlean (Meryl Streep) ponders her own lack of passion, as realized through her profile of John Laroche.*

adaptation of Orlean's book, and by extension of any literary text, is a contradiction in terms."[11] In discussing the film, Leitch highlights how *Adaptation.* does push its deconstructive impulses to an unprecedented limit, but it also belongs to a long tradition of reflexive metafiction that highlights its own storytelling and adaptation processes, citing similar examples of films such as *Shadow of the Vampire* (E. Elias Merhige, 2000), *Looking for Richard* (Al Pacino, 1996), *Jane Austen in Manhattan* (James Ivory, 1980), and *A Cock and Bull Story* (Michael Winterbottom, 2005). As Leitch writes, "Despite their many differences, all these films deconstruct the mimetic illusion by examining the problems of arranging or staging preexisting material for the theater or the cinema."[12] Through its engagement with such reflexive tropes and strategies, *Adaptation.* finds itself in a small but recognizable subgenre of metafictional adaptations.

But unlike all of the examples Leitch mentions, *Adaptation.* is notable for being based on a nonfiction source, raising ethical issues as discussed in Chapter 1. Typical nonfiction adaptations need to consider the ethics of dramatizing events whose truth value may be unknown or clearly constructed for dramatic convenience, but *Adaptation.* takes fictionalization far beyond such typical techniques, turning the author of its nonfiction source into a drug-crazed kidnapper and killing off the book's main character. Clearly this would be regarded as unethical if it were being done seriously without the consent of Orlean and Laroche, portraying them as criminals and asserting that *The Orchid Thief* lies about their real motives and activities. The film's comedic tone provides a rationale for such extreme exaggerations and fictionalization, and Orlean approved the use of her name for her nonrealistic characterization. However, the film flouts and rebukes the norms of adaptation and fidelity for satirical purposes in ways that might be hard to comprehend for the casual first-time viewer.

One of ways that the film challenges viewers is by not clearly demarcating the difference between what is fictional and factual throughout, leaving it somewhat difficult to discern what is based on reality versus completely fictional. However, *Adaptation.* does follow some subtle textual patterns that help us chart the difference between fact and fiction throughout. For the first two-thirds of the film, nearly everything we see and hear in the storyline between Susan and John is taken from Orlean's book, and thus is presumably factual; additionally, all of these scenes take place in the past, before the book was published. Additionally, the film's other moments that take place prior to the main plot line of Charlie writing his screenplay are factual, such as the evolution montage or the scene of Darwin writing his book. Thus *Adaptation.* structures its presentation of fact temporally, providing consistency by defining everything we see that chronologically precedes Charlie's opening scene as rooted in reality. The unusual final act takes Susan and Laroche's story into the present day, signaling that it no longer belongs to the past tense of Orlean's factual reporting and embracing the realm of fictional Hollywood filmmaking.

The film's main storyline with Charlie attempting to write a screenplay is much more thoroughly fictionalized, although rooted in some factual basis. The real Charlie Kaufman did struggle with the process of adapting *The Orchid Thief* while *Being John Malkovich* was shooting, and Kaufman was only able to succeed by writing himself and his struggles into the screenplay. However, the character of Charlie diverges significantly from the real Kaufman—although they might share some tendency toward depressive self-loathing, Charlie is far more exaggerated in his misery, and the real Kaufman was married with a daughter at the time of *Adaptation.*, rather than frustratingly searching for love. Most vitally, Charlie Kaufman has no twin brother, as the character of Donald is the only completely fictional figure among the film's main characters, and he functions as the agent of fictionalization and exaggeration throughout the film.

Donald's presence for the first seventy-five minutes is primarily a foil to Charlie, serving as a point of contrast in terms of screenwriting style and success, as well as his romantic success in quickly developing a relationship with

Caroline while Charlie struggles to connect with Amelia. In the pivotal turning point triggering the final act, Charlie brings Donald to New York to help him develop the script, a crucial narrative development that transforms Susan's storyline into the realm of fiction. The first time we see Susan behave in a way fully distinct from her book's account is when Donald, pretending to be Charlie, goes to interview her in at her *New Yorker* office. While there is nothing directly indicating that this is a fictionalization, Donald takes her answers as an indication that she is covering something up, a suspicion that he confirms when he sees an image of Susan naked on Laroche's pornographic website—the real Laroche did run a porn site according to *The Orchid Thief*, but there is no reason to suspect that Orlean ever appeared there outside of the fictional realm of *Adaptation.* This revelation is followed by a scene in the swamp where Laroche and Susan find a ghost orchid, with her voice-over—the first that does not quote her book—admitting deceit: "I lied about my change. I lied in my book. I pretended with my husband that everything was the same, but something happened in the swamp that day" (80). Susan's first encounter with Donald triggers a divergence from the nonfiction of her book, as the film claims that the book is a lie and takes her story down an outrageous fictionalized path of orchid-derived drugs, adultery, car chases, and murder. Thus Donald is the catalyst of transforming nonfiction into fiction, jettisoning fidelity by adapting Orlean's real reporting into unreal Hollywood storytelling, a crucial role that requires us to explore the concept of character in more depth.

Comprehending *Adaptation.*'s complex characters

In most films, characters function exclusively as agents within the fictional world, carrying out the plot and captivating viewer attention, allegiance, and engagement. *Adaptation.* adds two important layers to that function: as with most nonfiction adaptations, many of the film's characters are representations of real-life people, and thus viewers consider the degree to which their on-screen and offscreen personas reconcile. Less typically, many of *Adaptation.*'s main characters are also storytellers, and thus are imbricated into the creation of the narrative we are watching, adding a far more complex and reflexive function to our processes of character comprehension. To make sense of these multiple functions, we need to use theoretical concepts of characterization as outlined in Chapter 1.

Murray Smith's three levels of character recognition, alignment, and allegiance are useful to make sense of the film's character constellations, although allegiance is not particularly relevant to the film's narrative strategies.[13] As mentioned above, *Adaptation.* tackles one aspect of character recognition head-on, by using performance, costuming, and dialogue to make sure viewers can easily keep twin brothers Charlie and Donald distinct despite both being portrayed by Cage; this clarity of recognition is motivated by the film's desire to provide contrast between the two, rather than blur their identities. Instead, the more nuanced issues concerning recognition involve the boundary between a real person and their cinematic character. Notably, none of the real people representing in the film are particularly famous or recognizable—the three best-known people dramatized are Charlie Kaufman, Susan Orlean, and Robert McKee, all of whom were much better known for the words they had written rather than their physical appearance or personalities. McKee was probably best known as a figure in 2002, as many aspiring screenwriters had attended his seminars; reportedly, Brian Cox's performance captured the real McKee's blustery lecturing style, persona, and appearance enough to feel accurate to viewers who had experience with the real person. Cox, who at the time was a successful but not high-profile film character actor and a prominent stage actor in Britain, would not be highly recognizable to most viewers, so his performance feels "true" to the real person, with little in his scenes to suggest that the character misrepresents the real McKee.

Unlike Cox, both Nicolas Cage and Meryl Streep were highly prominent film actors in 2002, making them far more recognizable as stars than the real-life figures they portray. Even though few viewers have specific knowledge of what the real Kaufman and Orlean look like or how they behave, we never forget that we are watching award-winning actors play these characters, as the film does little to make the actors appear like the real people, such as dying Streep's hair to match the redheaded Orlean, or casting actors who resemble their real subjects. Their performances as Charlie and Susan feel more like *performances*, rather than dramatizations of real people (as with Cox's McKee), a choice that makes sense given the degree to which their stories in *Adaptation.* greatly diverge from the real lives of Kaufman and Orlean. Chris Cooper's portrayal of John Laroche similarly feels like a performance, even though Cooper was far less known than Cage or Streep at the time; however, the real Laroche was only notable through his profile in Orlean's writing, and thus Cooper's performance created the public image of the person. Within the film, Valerie comments how Laroche is "a fun character," which Laroche agrees with, and asserts that "I think I should play me," thus reinforcing the blur between performance and real figure (61).

Adaptation.'s three main characters based on real people all allow their on-screen performances to define them, thus allowing their fictionalization and portrayal of highly unreal narrative events to feel consistent with the film's tone. This approach contrasts with how the film presents other real figures, namely the actors from *Being John Malkovich*. From the opening sequence featuring Malkovich on-set, to a brief nonspeaking cameo by John Cusack, to Charlie's jealousy that Donald is playing Boggle with Catherine Keener at his house, the well-known actors from Kaufman and Jonze's first film briefly appear in this film as themselves, calling attention to *Adaptation.*'s partial grounding in the real world where these actors co-exist with screenwriter Charlie Kaufman. Cusack, Malkovich, and Cage had all appeared together on-screen previously in *Con Air* (Simon West, 1997), highlighting how

Cage's role in *Adaptation.* differs from their appearances—instead of three Hollywood stars all playing fictional roles or appearing as themselves, Cage embodies the fictionalized Charlie and utterly fictional Donald, while his two former costars play themselves. This contrast highlights the cognitive processes of recognition that viewers engage in when watching such a multilayered representation as in *Adaptation.*, as we must work to differentiate between well-known actors playing themselves, playing real people like Charlie, and playing fictional figures like Donald, an ongoing process that becomes more complicated as the on-screen events become increasingly outlandish toward the film's end.

If character recognition forces us to engage with layers of fact and fiction, the concept of character alignment highlights the operational dimension of storytelling. At the most basic level, we are aligned with Charlie for most of the film, placing us alongside him as he struggles to write his script, yearns for Amelia, rereads *The Orchid Thief* for inspiration, and masturbates to fantasies of both professional and personal satisfaction. Almost all of the film's scenes feature Charlie, or are dramatized from his reading of Orlean's book—one of the very few moments before the film's final act that is not aligned with Charlie is when Susan and Valerie meet to discuss her book being optioned, a scene that clearly implicates Charlie even as it does not immediately feature him (although he does arrive in the restaurant in a later scene that continues from this moment). Beyond that scene, every other moment aligns us with Charlie, either directly or via the once-removed experience of Orlean's book, sharing his knowledge, attitudes, internal thoughts and fantasies, and experiences—until the film's transformed final act.

Once Donald joins Charlie in New York to trigger the final act, *Adaptation.*'s pattern of alignment shifts away from Charlie toward embracing a more wide-ranging and conventional perspective. Pretending to be Charlie, Donald goes to interview Susan in the film's only moment of mistaken twin identity (although viewers are never confused about their identities), and the first break from being aligned with Charlie. That scene is soon followed by the first flashback that is clearly not from Orlean's book: Susan admits to lying in the book as she and John find a ghost orchid, and for more than seven minutes, we follow their flashback that reveals their "real" bond over the orchid-derived drug that "helps people be fascinated" to solve Susan's longing for passion (81). This shift in alignment signals a new relationship between character and storytelling for the final act, abandoning's both Charlie's perspective and the fidelity to *The Orchid Thief* for all flashbacks, exchanging them for an infusion of Hollywood conventions and dramatic inventions as provided by Donald's influence. While these scenes are not aligned with Donald as a character, they are aligned with him as a storyteller, highlighting that character in *Adaptation.* matters at levels of both story and discourse.

This shift highlights one of the most unusual aspects of *Adaptation.*'s approach to storytelling, characters, and narrators. In typical instances where a character functions as a narrator, we expect that their perspective will color the interpretation and presentation of the story—they might withhold particular information, offer commentary on events, or in the case of unreliable narration, even deceive readers or viewers about what really happened. However, in all of those instances, we assume that there is a baseline of events that "really" happened within the storyworld, and that the narrator is only impacting our knowledge of and access to those events through the narrative discourse. In *Adaptation.*, however, the characters who function as narrators are constructing the story events as well as the discourse. For the first two-thirds of the film, Charlie stays true to the events told in *The Orchid Thief*, and the storylines about his own writer's block and romantic troubles seem to be "real" within the film's storyworld; Charlie's main deviation from conventional narration is his decision to write himself into his screenplay, which results in the very film we are watching. However, Donald's efforts are much more radical in approach even as they hew more to Hollywood conventions: his influence in the final act overhauls the real-life events from the book and the subsequent lives of Orlean and Laroche, as well as reversing narrative information established earlier in the film. Donald's presence as storyteller reshapes the story in unexpected ways that seem to manipulate other characters and events, rather than just manage information or deceive us.

Is this a case of unreliable narration? Not in typical terms, as unreliable narration involves misleading audiences about what "really" happened within the story. But are we to believe that the final events of John and Donald's deaths and Susan's arrest didn't really happen within *Adaptation.*'s story? We have no frame of reference to suggest otherwise, except our extratextual knowledge that none of those things happened to the real people that the film is based on—most cases of unreliable narration reveal their unreliability in a final twist that clarifies what was real and deception, but *Adaptation.* simply presents the narrative events of the final act as equally "real" as those based on its nonfiction source. Since unreliable narration normally highlights how the narrative presentation deviates from the truth of the story within the film's fiction, we have no reason to believe that these events did not happen, as we are given no alternative version. It would be fair to call the film an "unreliable adaptation" of *The Orchid Thief* and the real lives of Orlean and Laroche, but that unreliability is more about its story events rather than the narrative discourse. This distinction highlights how the characters of Charlie and Donald function less as narrators telling the story, but as authors who are creating the story—thus leading us to the final theoretical concept needed to make sense of the film, authorship.

Adaptation.'s active authors

As discussed in Chapter 1, film critics and scholars nearly always identify directors as authorial figures, responsible for the collaborative creative choices that produce a final film. Even though authorship emerges from literature and evokes the writing process, screenwriters are rarely accorded authorial status, except when a film is written and directed by the same person or team. *Adaptation.* is a notable exception, as Spike Jonze's authorial presence is notably absent from both the critical conversation around the film and within the film itself, overshadowed by the on-screen representation of the film's three credited writers. Understanding how *Adaptation.* asserts writers as authorial figures and downplays the role of the director helps us make sense of the film's narrative design and overall meanings.

The contrast between writer and director is established in the film's first scene: Charlie is asked to leave the set for the film he wrote for being "in the eyeline," making it quite clear that the screenwriter is more of a nuisance than welcome presence during a film's production. However, *Adaptation.* does not represent director Spike Jonze on-screen at all, choosing instead to feature other production crew that report to Jonze, the first assistant director and cinematographer. By conspicuously leaving Jonze offscreen, the film declines to overtly assert directorial authority, contrasting how other directors such as Alfred Hitchcock and M. Night Shyamalan appear in cameos in their films. Even though Charlie is marginalized within the production of *Being John Malkovich*, *Adaptation.* never offers images of another competing authorial figure, thus suggesting that Charlie does function as the author, even as he is being dismissed by the crew.

This authorial role is reinforced throughout the rest of *Adaptation.*'s representation of the creative processes of filmmaking, as the only people we ever see working to create the film version of *The Orchid Thief* are Charlie, Donald, Valerie, and Charlie's agent Marty, all of whom are involved in the preproduction process of writing and commissioning a screenplay. Throughout the film, we watch multiple writers at work: Charlie and Susan both write their works on-screen and narrate their writing via voice-over; Donald and Charlie discuss their writing content and process via dialogue; and McKee lectures a crowd of aspiring writers on the craft of storytelling. In contrast, we never see film directing or hear it discussed—in fact, we regularly hear Charlie describing his written sequences that we have already witnessed on-screen, subtly suggesting that a screenplay can be visualized and dramatized faithfully without an overt guiding directorial force. Through this emphasis on writing and omission of directing, *Adaptation.* posits a vision of the filmmaking process as the manifestation of a writer's thoughts on-screen, rather than an intensely collaborative effort helmed by a director. Additionally, the film is typically subdued visually, allowing its experimental impulses to be felt in the writing and structure, and thus downplaying the role of director as overt creative presence.

This screenwriter-centered representation of filmmaking is neither a mistake nor a romanticization by Kaufman and/or Jonze—interviews with both of them highlight their collaboration in making *Adaptation.* and clearly neither is naïve about the remarkable team effort needed to produce a movie. Jonze particularly is credited in interviews for his work with actors, establishing pacing in both shooting and editing, and collaborating with Kaufman on the film's structure. Instead, it is a highly strategic choice made by both writer and director to portray the characters who are writers as authorial agents and downplay the unrepresented director, working to evoke a viewer's understanding of writers guiding what we see and hear. Granting authorial power to writers is crucial to the film's design, as we watch the writing process reflexively construct the very film we are watching. This "instant production" ignores the actual mechanics of filmmaking that we see represented on the *Malkovich* set and the essential postproduction processes of editing and sound mixing, leaving the false impression that once writers put ideas on the page, they become manifest on film. But which writers have this power?

Four characters in the film are writers, and all have a hand in guiding *Adaptation.*'s storytelling. Clearly Charlie embodies the film's authorial role most directly: his story is literally the story of the film's writing. There is never any doubt that

Charlie serves an authorial role for the film, as we are quick to elide the distinction between the fictionalized Charlie and the real Kaufman by witnessing Charlie construct the story we are viewing and connecting that practice and identity to the real screenwriter. Susan's authorial role is foregrounded as well, with her clearly creating the source material that forms the basis for the film; as discussed above, the use of her voice-over reading lines from the book and visualized scenes from her reporting emphasize her authorial role. Thus the characters of Charlie and Susan mirror the real Kaufman and Orlean, who serve both real and dramatized roles of adapting screenwriter and nonfiction book writer respectively, thereby infusing the characters with authorial agency.

The other two writer-characters are more complicated to locate as authors, but serve roles vital to understanding the narrative. Robert McKee is portrayed as both a writer and teacher of writing, represented in the film both lecturing to aspiring writers and clearly identified as the author of the book *Story*. McKee is figured as parallel to Susan Orlean as authors of books, seen in the scene where Charlie and Donald lie in adjacent hotel beds reading *Story* and *The Orchid Thief*

FIGURE 2.4 *Charlie and Donald Kaufman (Nicolas Cage) read* Story *and* The Orchid Thief *respectively.*

respectively. Quotations from *Story* appear in the film, both as quoted by Donald and spoken by McKee in his seminar, and clearly his influence greatly shapes *Adaptation.*'s final act. However, McKee lacks the agency of the film's other writer-characters, as he is never seen writing nor taking a direct hand in shaping the film's storytelling. Instead, he serves as inspiring source material, making the film partly an indirect adaptation of *Story*—or to use its own biological metaphors, we might view *Adaptation.* as a cross-pollination between *The Orchid Thief* and *Story*.

It takes Donald to germinate this hybrid species, as he becomes the agent that allows McKee's influence to bloom. We witness Donald writing his own screenplay, as his progress laps the more experienced Charlie, and we are regularly reminded of his knack for dramatic structure and embrace of commercially viable conventions. The film's final act commences when Charlie invites Donald to New York, and asks, "How would the great Donald end this script?" (74), formally granting Donald authorial power. As discussed above, this shift realigns the film to Donald as storyteller, changing the style of the narrative discourse to fit his more plot-driven, externalized approach to filmmaking versus Charlie's interior reflexive tone. Once Donald takes the reins of the storytelling, *Adaptation.* stops being about the process of writing a film and becomes more of a mystery/thriller (per Donald's favored genre) focused on uncovering the "truth" about Susan and John. Because Donald's tone is less reflexive and focuses on story events over discourse, the film does not overtly signal handing off the authorial mantle as clearly as one might expect, leading many viewers to miss the transition and be confused as to why the film's final act is so unlike what preceded it.

To fully understand this narrative transition, viewers need to draw upon the concept of the implied author, attributing filmmaking choices and storytelling to an imaginary authorial figure. For the first two-thirds of the film, *Adaptation.* is full of reflexive cues that guide viewers to conceive of this implied author as the fictional Charlie, with Susan functioning as a secondary implied author of the segments adapted from her book. It is hard to imagine watching these first seventy-five minutes without imagining Charlie as the film's author, as we regularly watch him author the footage we have seen and call attention to how he has written himself into his script. As we watch the film unfold, we connect the character of Charlie to a mental construct of the real Kaufman, constituting the figure of the implied author. Even though the real Charlie Kaufman was virtually unknown to most viewers in 2002, his on-screen avatar provides sufficient material to allow audiences to imagine the real Kaufman authoring the film and guiding the narrative. *Adaptation.* discourages us from thinking about the film's narration as stemming just from an impersonal cinematic system, as per David Bordwell's theory discussed in Chapter 1, but rather it constantly encourages us to personalize the narration as tied to Charlie Kaufman as its implied author.[14]

The final act's tonal transformation encourages viewers to engage with the operational aesthetic and ask questions about the film's storytelling: what happened to prompt this radical shift? The answer—Donald has taken over writing the film—disrupts our notion of the implied author for the rest of *Adaptation.* But since the authorial mantle is passed with some subtlety, many viewers may be slow to notice the shift; certainly the more obvious explanation for the transformed final act is that Charlie took McKee's advice to heart and radically overhauled his writing style. Yet this seems both completely inconsistent with Charlie's character, who is both highly committed to his artistic values and paralyzed by fear of change, and overlooks that Donald plays a more important role in the film's final act, rarely leaving Charlie's side until his death. Instead, engaged viewers need to connect the implausible story events with the shifting character roles, tone, and notions of authorial presence.

As discussed in Chapter 1, the implied author function is dependent on viewers bringing knowledge and cues from outside the story to construct an image of authorial figures to guide the storytelling. In *Adaptation.*, there are no paratexts about Donald Kaufman to draw upon outside the film, since he is a wholly fictional creation. And yet there are two small cues within the film yet outside its story that highlight Donald's role. The first is the unusual opening credit that lists Donald as co-screenwriter, which, as discussed above, required the producers to petition the Writer's Guild for permission to credit the film to a fictional character. The reason the filmmakers were willing to go through that hassle was that it was imperative to comprehending the film—we need to know that Donald cowrote the script for the shifting implied author to make sense for the film's final act. The film simply does not make much sense if we imagine that it is solely Charlie's creation—it is fine to know that the actual script was solely written by the real Charlie Kaufman (building off Orlean's book), but his screenplay creates dual implied authors as embodied in the film's twin characters. The second cue comes at the end of the closing credits, with the dedication "In Loving Memory of Donald Kaufman," signaling Donald's existence outside of the film's fiction and further validating his authorial role. These credits do not require viewers to believe that Donald is based on a real person like Charlie or Susan, but rather perpetuate the sense that Donald's presence matters as more than just comic relief and a contrasting foil for Charlie within the film's story—his role in the film's storytelling is affirmed by these elements that reach beyond the fictional story.

While *Adaptation.* is far from a mystery as a film, it does create an enigma in its final act, shifting storytelling styles and story content in ways that belie an obvious interpretation. The film asks viewers to analyze its narrative techniques to make sense of what happens and uncover the perpetrator as Donald, the implied coauthor. To comprehend its storytelling, the film demands that we draw upon narrative theory, ranging from the concept of act structure discussed by McKee in the film, to notions of authorship and character that are alluded to throughout. Many of these theoretical ideas require no training beyond paying close attention to the film and being familiar with conventions of filmmaking, but hopefully this detailed analysis highlights how important theoretical concepts are to being able to both comprehend and appreciate *Adaptation.* as a film.

But what about *The Three*?

While we may have solved the film's main mystery, there is another tied to Donald's character and authorial role. *Adaptation.* clearly engages with other written works, most directly Orlean's *The Orchid Thief* and McKee's *Story*, representing both books on-screen and dramatizing ideas and passages directly from their pages. Charlie's adapted script, which we see and hear in progress throughout the film, is also a key part of the film's narrative, forming the basis for the drama we are witnessing and reflexively serving as the foundational material for the film itself. But one other written document is prominently featured in the film and deserves some consideration: Donald's original screenplay, *The Three*. To unpack the narrative function of this script and consider its importance to our understanding and appreciation of its role in the film, we need to use all of the tools in our narrative theory toolbox, and thus it serves as an apt conclusion for this extended narrative analysis of *Adaptation.*

One of the film's more hidden enigmas comes at the end of its closing credits. Right before the dedication to the memory of Donald, an unusual quotation appears on-screen:

> "We're all one thing, Lieutenant. That's what I've come to realize. Like cells in a body. 'Cept we can't see the body. The way fish can't see the ocean. And so we envy each other. Hurt each other. Hate each other. How silly is that? A heart cell hating a lung cell." – Cassie from *The Three*

This is the only direct quote we ever get from Donald's script, and it comes at a closing moment in the film's credits that few viewers will likely ever see. Yet it was clearly designed to be there, as both the quotation and the dedication to Donald are the only credits written directly into the film's screenplay (100). Thus we should take its inclusion as a signal that there is something worth thinking about regarding *The Three* and its relationship to the larger film.

Donald's thriller, about a cop, a serial killer, and a female victim who all turn out to be the same person with multiple personality disorder, is clearly a satirical jab at "puzzle films" with big twists that were prominent in the late-1990s, such as *The Sixth Sense* (M. Night Shyamalan, 1999), *Fight Club* (David Fincher, 1999), *Memento* (Christopher Nolan, 2000), *The Usual Suspects* (Bryan Singer, 1995), and *Dark City* (Alex Proyas, 1998). Donald's plot summary is purposely incoherent, a fact that only Charlie (and the audience) can recognize, and thus serves as a way for Kaufman to distinguish his brand of reflexive filmmaking from other experimental styles of the time. But that doesn't mean that *The Three* is only there as a joke, as placing the quotation in the final credits would not make much sense if only to remind us that Donald wrote a hackneyed thriller. If Donald's script were only in the film to represent the epitome of Hollywood stupidity, it could have been about anything. But instead it is about a trio of characters—two male, one female—who appear to be distinct, but are ultimately revealed to be one and the same. *Adaptation.* is also about a trio of writers—two male, one female—who appear to be different, but share the ultimate identity of joint authors of the fiction we are viewing. This thematic and structural resonance points toward the significance of *The Three.*

As discussed above, understanding *Adaptation.* requires viewers to be consciously engaged with thinking about authorship, constructing an implied authorial presence that guides our interpretation of the film. The film's three credited writers might be thought of as metaphorically paralleling the multiple personalities of *The Three*'s protagonist. The film's reflexivity invites us, via the operational aesthetic, to think of the storytelling itself as part of its drama and plot. Since the film's plot centers around Charlie's struggle to write its own script, the mystery of *The Three* grounds that goal as the internal struggle between three facets of the same figure. Thus we might reconceive the protagonist of *Adaptation.* not as Charlie as a character, but as its implied author; that figure is not limited to the singular character of Charlie, but vacillates between the three personalities and storytelling styles of Charlie, Susan, and Donald throughout the film as they alternate taking control of the narrative. If the big twist of *The Three* is the revelation that all three characters are identical, then *Adaptation.* offers a parallel final act transformation by incorporating Donald into the three-headed authorial figure.

The importance of *The Three* shines through other facets of narrative theory beyond character and authorship as well. Clearly narrative structure and practical theory as essential to both understanding *Adaptation.* and to the success of *The Three* within the film's story, as the brothers' agent Marty first encourages Charlie to enlist Donald's help by touting how "he's really goddamned amazing at structure" (65). Although it is highly unconventional, *Adaptation.* is also highly dependent on structure, using the film's act segments to establish, develop, and transform its reflexive complexities in narrative discourse without becoming incoherent or confusing. While *The Three* is predicated on revealing its complexity through a final twist within its storyworld, *Adaptation.*'s final act transformation is tied to its narrative discourse. Both scripts rely on the conventions of practical theory to produce unconventional results, and in doing so, parallel how conventions might be connected to originality in both premise and execution.

The concept of adaptation might also pertain to *The Three*. In *Adaptation.*, Donald dies tragically after being shot by Laroche and flung through the windshield in the climactic car chase, leaving behind a "posthumous" co-writing credit for his brother's adapted screenplay, as well as his own unproduced script of *The Three*. But through the parallels between those two scripts, in their play with McKee's conventions and focus on three characters serving as facets of the same figure—the killer in *The Three*, the implied author in *Adaptation.*—might we think of *The Three* as yet another source for *Adaptation.*? Just as McKee's *Story* functions as uncredited source material that helps shape *Adaptation.*, so does *The Three*, enough to inspire the real Kaufman to include a quotation from the script before a tribute to his (fictional) twin brother. While *The Three* does not really exist outside of *Adaptation.*'s own storyworld, it exerts a powerful influence on the film, reflexively functioning as part of the source material for its own creation.

Or perhaps it's just a joke. One of the beauties of *Adaptation.*'s playful reflexivity is that it can simultaneously embrace levels of metafiction and thematic resonance, and also make fun of itself. As film viewers and critics, we can do the same through applying theory to our analysis: we should take these concepts seriously and strive to make deeper sense of films that fascinate and entertain us, but we should also have fun with our own critical practice, making the process of analysis itself playfully reflexive. That seems like a good final takeaway from both the film and our analysis of it through the lens of narrative theory.

Notes

1 Susan Orlean, "Orchid Fever," *The New Yorker*, January 23, 1995; Susan Orlean, *The Orchid Thief* (New York: Random House, 1998).

2 See Jonathan Gray, *Show Sold Separately: Promos, Spoilers, and Other Media Paratexts* (New York: New York University Press, 2010).

3 All quotations from *Adaptation.* are referenced from Charlie Kaufman and Donald Kaufman, Adaptation.: *The Shooting Script* (New York: Newmarket Press, 2002), 1.

4 Blake Snyder, *Save the Cat! The Last Book on Screenwriting You'll Ever Need* (Studio City, CA: Michael Wiese Productions, 2005), 72.

5 In discussing the overlapping characters and writers in this book, I will refer to the real-life individuals by their last names (Kaufman, Orlean), and their fictionalized characters by first names (Charlie, Susan). Since Donald Kaufman has no real-life counterpart, he will only be referenced as Donald.

6 McKee, *Story*, 46.

7 Ibid., 86.

8 Ibid., 402.

9 Ibid., 221.

10 Ibid., 46.

11 Leitch, *Film Adaptation and Its Discontents*, 111–12.

12 Ibid., 112.

13 Murray Smith, *Engaging Characters: Fiction, Emotion, and the Cinema* (New York: Oxford University Press, USA, 1995).

14 David Bordwell, *Narration in the Fiction Film* (Madison: University of Wisconsin Press, 1985), 62.

Conclusion

Perhaps after thousands of words and countless claims, it may seem like there is nothing more to say about *Adaptation.* However, film scholars rarely run out of things to say about any given film, especially one as complex and distinctive as *Adaptation.* We have, perhaps, reached the limit of what narrative theory can tell us about the film, at least on its own. For most film scholars, a single theoretical school is not the sole source of inspiration or framework to analyze a text, as they tend to draw upon multiple theories and perspectives to make sense of a given example. This conclusion offers brief explorations of how we might use other theoretical perspectives in conjunction with narrative theory to analyze *Adaptation.*, suggesting how any film can benefit by being analyzed through a range of theoretical lenses—these short discussions are not meant to be full-fledged analyses, but rather point toward the approaches and issues that such analyses might take if developed further.

The cultural politics of *Adaptation.*

As discussed earlier in the book, narrative theory does not primarily concern itself with analyzing what a given text means, but instead explores how it makes meaning and tells stories. But narrative theory can still be quite useful to help interpret and analyze meanings, providing insights into a text that help us make sense of it. In the previous chapter, narrative theory pointed toward how *Adaptation.* structures themes of creativity, passion, and desire into its storytelling, and how *The Three* functions as a parallel narrative to the film's main story. Such interpretations might be interesting to understand some of the film's creative design and commentary about the artistry and craft of filmmaking, but such thematic analysis is rarely the goal of theoretically inflected scholarly criticism. Instead, most film theories strive to connect the meanings of films with broader social and cultural systems of power and identity.

One of the major underlying theoretical paradigms that runs throughout film studies is *ideology theory*. In brief, theories of ideology strive to understand how cultural forms like popular cinema work to maintain dominant power relations, ranging from economic inequality to norms of race and gender. The crucial insight of ideology theory is that popular culture works to normalize the status quo and make the dominant systems of power invisible and unquestioned, integrated into a viewer's common sense and outlook on the world. Film scholars have explored how conventions of filmmaking, from industry structure to norms of narrative and style, work to reinforce dominant ideology in both overt and subtle ways. *Adaptation.* features many norms that might be regarded as reinforcing dominant ideology, while seemingly challenging others, and thus an ideological approach informed by narrative theory can help us understand various facets of the film.

For the most devout ideological critics, nearly all conventional films work to reinforce dominant ideology, even when they seem to offer critique or resistance. *Adaptation.* would seem to fit this latter category, given that the film makes fun of Hollywood filmmaking and thus it might critically question how typical films function as ideology, such as with Charlie's objections about how Hollywood conventions construct a world where problems can be neatly solved within two hours and people are able to effectively take action to better themselves. Such storytelling norms certainly contradict the complexities of the real world, where people cannot necessarily control their own stories and are beset by more complicated problems that are structured by unequal systems of power. However, even as he tries to resist narrative conventions, Charlie's stated goals of representing Orlean's beautiful observations about nature and passion do not challenge dominant power structures—instead, both Susan and Charlie are lodged within a normative perspective where they write from a position of wealth and privilege, ignoring the unequal social structures that enable them to worry about flowers and creative freedoms instead of fighting more widespread battles for social justice or equality. *Adaptation.* seems utterly uninterested in challenging or even mentioning dominant norms of power and wealth, even as it resists conventional storytelling techniques, thereby reinforcing ideologies as unspoken common sense. Additionally, the film's final swerve into Hollywood convention gently satirizes the norms, but ultimately validates them by allowing Charlie to learn, change, and succeed by sacrificing both his brother's life and his inflexible artistic ideals, rather than offering a clear condemnation of commercial filmmaking that would be needed to resist dominant ideology.

Such extreme ideological readings can easily reach their limits, as ultimately everything might just boil down to demonstrating how every example of commercial culture reinforces dominant norms—that is certainly true to a point, but such insights can lack nuance or specificity. As such, few academic critics merely point out hidden ideologies embedded in films, but rather highlight how such ideologies function within film storytelling, visual style, or other methods of normalizing and reinforcing the status quo within a broader cultural system of power and inequality. Typically, such analysis works best by looking at larger patterns of meaning rather than analyzing a single film; we might look at *Adaptation.* in context of other representations of the film industry from the era, such as *Mulholland Drive* (David Lynch, 2001) and *State and Main* (David Mamet, 2000), to explore how such films reinforce unspoken norms about Hollywood and mainstream culture, even as they position themselves as critiques.

Other incarnations of ideology theory draw upon psychoanalytic traditions to dive deeper into the unconscious ways that such norms are perpetuated or challenged, typically through the manifestation of desire, establishment of identification, and reliance on voyeurism. *Psychoanalytic film theory* is quite complex and it is difficult to briefly sketch out what such critics might make of a text as reflexive and self-aware as *Adaptation.*; however, we can see some useful connections that point toward a more elaborated analysis. Per some psychoanalytic critics, films create a dreamlike fantasy that unconsciously inscribes viewers into dominant ideology, identifying with idealized screen protagonists and encouraging us to imagine our worlds as complete and fulfilling as popular cinema represents. *Adaptation.* seems to counter such an impulse, as Charlie's self-loathing encourages us to disidentify with him, and his inability to fulfill his goals violates the norms of Hollywood filmmaking—instead he is literally a divided subject, fractured into dual twins to dramatize his inner psychological strife. However, the conventional conclusion could be seen as the fantasy overtaking reality, reinforcing that despite the film's critique of Hollywood fantasy, that fantasy is ultimately what wins out in the end and validates our pleasure in the ending that "wows" us, per McKee's edict, killing Donald and unifying Charlie's subjectivity.

One crucial concept within psychoanalytic film theory is desire, the overriding unconscious impulse that drives people, and that films unleash their psychological power by making desires manifest on-screen through fantasy. Unlike most films, however, *Adaptation.* explores desire more consciously and reflexively, as Charlie's struggle is explicitly framed as his dual desires for sexual connection (to Amelia or the other women he fantasizes about) and creative completion of his screenplay, and Susan's meditations on orchids revolve around her desire for passion using sexual metaphors and references to flowers. For most of the film, desire is frequently discussed and portrayed, whether through Charlie's masturbatory fantasies or Susan's eloquent descriptions of John's passion for collecting orchids, but it is far from unconscious or even felt by spectators—the film's first two-thirds do not elicit the typical emotional connections that drive narrative cinema, as we watch as amused but detached viewers curiously trying to figure out the film's underlying logic and learning about orchids. The final act's shift to narrative convention embraces the typical emotional connection to characters and suspenseful plotting, moving desire out of the conscious realm of dialogue and into the unconscious motives of characters and rhythms of climactic action. To better understand how the film might work to engage us in its reflexive fantasy, we could combine the tools of psychoanalytic and narrative theories if we wished to explore a more in-depth analysis.

One of the most influential incarnations of psychoanalytic theory is through its mixture with *feminist film theory*, focusing on how cinematic structures reinforce dominant gender relations and reduce women to the object of the male gaze—this theoretical model dominated much of film theory in the 1970s and 1980s, and although it has become more disputed and less prevalent in recent years, it is still relevant to some critics. *Adaptation.* certainly features moments of such a male gaze, especially as we ride along with Charlie's sexual fantasies about Susan, Valerie, and especially Alice, which features a gratuitous shot of the minor character topless. While conventional films typically represent such fantasies or sexualized scenes of protagonists' romantic conquests as highly desirable points of identification, *Adaptation.* works to undermine Charlie's desires as pathetic and more deserving of scorn than admiration—each sequence ends with the shame of Charlie alone in his room, frustrated in his masturbatory efforts, and thus may seem to critique such sexist voyeurism and viewers' own subsequent fantasies. Nonetheless, the camera still frames women on-screen via a male gaze, highlighting their physical attractiveness and roles as Charlie's objects of desire, while men are highlighted as unattractive and awkward. Aside from Susan, none of the film's female characters have any independent agency or characterization aside from their personal or professional relationship to Charlie, reinforcing the dominant role of men at the center of the film's universe.

Likewise, heterosexuality is so thoroughly normalized that no character is represented as gay, lesbian, or any other sexuality aside from assumed to be straight—such unrepresented sectors of sexual identity reinforce heterosexuality as the unspoken norm, as few people would think to analyze the film's homogenous representations of sexual orientation. Thus feminist theory can highlight the way that *Adaptation.* structures straight male identity as the dominant ideological norm, even as it does not seem to be a film "about" gender representations in any overt way; such is the power of ideological norms, as they reinforce themselves even when they do not seem to be the "point" of such representations.

Another relevant theoretical hybrid explores gender and narrative: *feminist narratology* considers how narrative theory's study of storytelling structure might be reconsidered in the light of gender norms and practices. More than looking at the representations found within a film's content, feminist narratology examines how gender plays out in both narrative form and reception practices—for instance, via the use of sentimentality, empathy, and repetition in traditionally feminine forms like melodrama and soap operas. *Adaptation.*'s formal features are quite unique and distinctive, but they are also typically masculine in following patterns and themes linked to male creators and consumers. The modernist impulse toward reflexivity and telling the story of tortured struggling (yet brilliant) creators has primarily been the realm of male artists, placing Kaufman alongside earlier lauded authorial figures like Fellini and Nabokov. It is particularly telling that Kaufman takes Orlean's book, about a female author exploring the life of a male subject and his obsessions, and makes it about himself—clearly the reflexive structure and his self-multiplication via his fictional twin reframe Orlean's work into a highly masculine realm. Such accounts of masculine and feminine norms of narrative structure are not meant to be totalizing or essentialist, as obviously individual men and women can tell stories in a wide range of ways; rather, feminist narratology recognizes that certain patterns and norms are typically tied to gender identities, and often appeal to particular audiences along a gendered divide.

Another key facet of film analysis that intertwines with studying gender is *critical race theory*, where racial identity might be examined both via on-screen representations and as part of the culture of media production. *Adaptation.* appears to be a highly homogenous film, with white people portraying nearly every character and serving as all major creative forces behind the scenes (as well as all of the filmmaking roles represented on-screen). As a film that does not seem to be "about" race, it would be tempting to say that issues of racial identity are irrelevant to understanding the film; however, one of the tenets of critical race theory is that all racial representations and categories, including those of whiteness, need to be analyzed to fully understand the intersections between race and social power. Thus we might look at how *Adaptation.*'s representations of whiteness, like its portrayal of characters with sufficient wealth and success to struggle with trying to tell the story of flowers, paint an ideal portrait of American privilege in which racial difference is nearly absent and nobody struggles with discrimination or limited access to be able to tell their stories. It would be quite a different film if it portrayed the struggles of a black screenwriter to get his film produced, given that Hollywood's rates of employment for nonwhite creative personnel are notoriously low. But as is, *Adaptation.* portrays a predominantly white, heterosexual male world of privilege, which frees it to address its less politicized themes of passion, creativity, and cinematic reflexivity. Analyzing absences is a key aspect of racial analysis, as visibility of marginalized groups is vital to understanding representation, as is the concept of *intersectionality*, which explores the conjuncture of multiple categories of identity, such as race, gender, and sexuality—notably, but not surprisingly for such a white and male-dominated film, *Adaptation.* features no representations of women of color aside from a few nonspeaking extras.

Despite the overwhelming whiteness of the main characters and milieu of the film, racial difference is crucial to John

Laroche's storyline: the real Laroche worked with a group of Seminole Indians to procure orchids from a Florida state preserve, using the legal loophole that allows Indians to violate state wildlife protections. *Adaptation.* represents Laroche's Seminole colleagues throughout the Florida sequences, although none are granted any real character development and only a few are even named or allowed to speak. One of the few moments where one of the Seminole characters is given significant dialogue comes when Susan comes to visit John at his nursery; after Matthew, one of John's Seminole colleagues, tells her that John is not there, he complements her hair, and then he flatly says, "I can see your sadness. It's lovely." After Susan awkwardly responds by asking Matthew for an interview for her story, he replies, "I'm not going to talk to you much. It's not personal. It's the Indian way" (22). This sequence, which is one of the very few Florida flashbacks not taken directly from Orlean's book, certainly plays upon racial stereotypes of Native Americans as both socially aloof and spiritually enlightened; importantly, Matthew's actions and dialogue do not develop his character in any way, as he never appears again with any significance.[1] Instead, his behavior functions to develop Susan's character, highlighting her discomfort with his actions and her own awkwardness with both her appearance and her spirituality. Thus the presence of Indian characters works as a contrasting "other" to provide insight into white characters, rather than actually developing fully realized nonwhite characters.

This use of Indians to reflect upon white characters is extended in the film's final act, as the storyline becomes increasingly sensational and clearly fictionalized, when John tells Susan that the stolen ghost orchids were actually used to produce a traditional Seminole ceremonial drug that the younger Indians used recreationally. When Susan asks whether Matthew was stoned when he seemed "fascinated" with her hair and sadness, John confirms that he "lived on that shit," and that the effect of the drug was to "help people be fascinated"—John offers to extract the drug for Susan, claiming "I'm probably the only white guy who knows" how to do it, explicitly naming his racial identity (81). Susan becomes enamored and possibly addicted to the drug, which fuels her rage when Charlie discovers their secret, highlighting her comparative inability to handle the drug's effects compared to the Seminoles. This sensational twist around drugs retroactively explains Matthew's behavior earlier in the film, although *Adaptation.*'s narrative structure suggests that developments in the Donald-authored final act are wholly fictionalized compared to the previous "real" representations of Florida stemming from Orlean's book. The introduction of Native drugs draws upon stereotypes of Indian rituals and use of hallucinogenic substances, but the film's reflexive conclusion seems to highlight how this is a hackneyed convention rather than a sincere representation of Seminole culture. Like much of *Adaptation.*, its use of Indian representations are quite ambiguous, straddling the line between offensive stereotype and reflexive critique of such racist shorthands. Understanding the politics of these representations requires more in-depth analysis of the film, its source material, and its broader social contexts.

These brief accounts of the film's ideology and representational politics might all seem to come together to attack *Adaptation.*, or serve primarily to point out its flaws. Do these approaches mean that it is a bad film, or cancel out the more positive impression that the previous chapter offered about its storytelling strategies and narrative innovations? Few film scholars are interested in reducing a film to simple binaries of good or bad, but rather are motivated to understand the complex and multifaceted ways that any film works, and how well it fulfills its design. Clearly *Adaptation.* was not designed to be a film about race or gender representation, nor even a political critique of Hollywood—instead, its aims are more focused around using innovative storytelling to represent creative practices, offer humorous commentary on Hollywood norms, and capture some of the themes of passion and desire via the discussions of nature found in Orlean's book. Narrative theory helps us understand how it does accomplish those goals admirably, and thus I would certainly assert that it is a highly successful film per its own design. However, that does not excuse its lack of critical perspective on its representational politics—just because it was not intended to be a film about race or gender, we should still be alert to and critical of its representations. Using film theory helps us hold multiple perspectives at the same time without resorting to a simplistic good/bad dichotomy: *Adaptation.* offers problematic and somewhat disappointing politics, while still being an impressively nuanced and successful narrative experiment. Thus we can celebrate a film's greatness while still acknowledging its flaws.

The cultural practices of *Adaptation.*

The various critical theories discussed above all analyze the film text itself as a site of meaning-making and interpretation. Other approaches to analyzing films expand the scope to consider the connections between a text and its broader cultural contexts. Such analyses typically fall under a broad approach known as *cultural studies*, which locates film and other media as part of a circuit of culture that charts the interactions between texts, production practices, media institutions, and audience reception practices. A cultural studies analysis stipulates that we cannot fully understand any film just by watching the film itself, but that we must always contextualize and draw connections between historically grounded cultural practices. Such practices are conceived as inherently plural rather than singular, highlighting how multiple inputs go into creating any text, and that consumers are bound to interpret a text in a wide range of ways depending on their social situations and personal histories. Cultural studies often intersects with other theoretical traditions, and thus critics might explore questions of representation or ideology, but by looking beyond the text to understand how the film's production and reception practices might inflect our analyses.

Adaptation. raises interesting questions about production practices, in large part because the film's reflexive portrayal of its own creation encourages us to think about how it came to be, and how its fictionalized representations might match or diverge from real practices. A study of the film's production practices requires research into materials beyond what is accessible from the officially released film, such as published interviews of creators, behind-the-scenes accounts by journalists, documentary footage of the production process, or interviewing cast and crew to hear perspectives from various people involved with the filmmaking process. Such a focus on the film's production practices highlights that any meanings found within the text do not stem from a single person's vision or intent, but rather are the by-product of a collaborative effort that is forged by multiple forces, goals, contexts, and choices, whether from authorial figures like director or writer, or crew members dedicated to particular cinematic elements, such as costume designers and editors.

One particular set of source materials that might shed light into *Adaptation.*, especially given its narrative focus on screenwriting and its privileging of writer as author, are multiple versions of the screenplay—we can compare the final published shooting script with two earlier drafts that are available to download online, as well as potentially other versions that might be obtained from production staff.[2] There are many significant differences between the available drafts and the final script, suggesting the influence of Spike Jonze and other collaborators in helping Charlie Kaufman modify his original vision of the screenplay, and complicating the idea that it emerges from a single (or triple, if we count Susan Orlean and Donald Kaufman) authorial voice. One telling revision concerns the vital transition into the film's final act: in the earliest available draft (labeled as "Second Draft" from September 1999), Donald answers Charlie's crucial question, "How would the great Donald end this script?," with much more explicit details, including the suggestion to "have some kind of bang-up, crazy action sequence in the swamp. Use the swamp better. It's a tremendous fictional world. A setting of great dramatic possibility" (94). Such explicit description of Donald's contributions to the script make the final act's authorial shift much more overt, reducing the subtlety and ambiguity found within the finished film. The earlier drafts also make the final act much more over-the-top in embracing Hollywood conventions, with extended dialogue between Charlie and Susan discussing the film's themes and lessons, a sudden appearance of a "swamp ape" monster (which is an actual Florida legend mentioned in *The Orchid Thief*), and a climax that results in Susan's death—heroically killed by Donald as his dying act in the first version, desperately committing suicide in the second. These earlier drafts call more attention to the boundaries between normal and excessive Hollywood conventions, suggesting how the filmmakers collaborated to rein in some of Kaufman's initial ideas in favor of the more naturalistic and subtle tone that appears in the final film.

Just as there are multiple layers of meaning-making that went into the creation of *Adaptation.*, viewers will certainly interpret and comprehend the film in a range of different ways. One of the key tenets of cultural studies is that we cannot discern audience interpretations from the film itself, but must look at actual viewers and their reception practices to understand how they engage with a text. We could certainly look at potential meanings that viewers could take from the text—for instance, we could imagine many viewers paying no attention to the representations of Native Americans discussed above, while others might regard them as demeaning and stereotypical, or perhaps some people might find them complimentary and accurate. Such interpretations are just hypothetical, however, and to really understand what viewers make of the film requires direct research into reception practices, such as by interviewing viewers or reading online discussion forums about the film.

This latter technique is quite accessible as a basic form of research that illuminates at least some viewer reactions, even if they are highly self-selecting and nonrepresentative. For instance, looking at the discussion thread on IMDB.com, we can see discussions debating the film's merits, and posing various interpretations and levels of narrative comprehension of its final act twist. For instance, one viewer started a thread called "Maybe it's me . . . I didn't get it," writing, "I found that the whole scenario with Meryl [*sic*] suggesting to kill Charlie came out of left field. I felt like I was watching a totally different movie." Other viewers weigh in to explain how Donald's influence took over in the final act, and argue the relative merits of the ending; one poster even asserts that the final act validates Donald as a writer: "At the same time it's sort of defending Donald's way of writing because the ending isn't all that bad and Charlie's big resolution in the third acting [*sic*] is actually a nice sentiment."[3] While we might think that the original poster misinterpreted the film by not understanding the authorial transition, clearly this is a fairly common reaction to the film, especially on the first viewing, and clearly not everyone appreciated the twist—as another viewer wrote, "I got it but it's too bad it wasn't worth getting." The point of such reception analysis is not to identify proper interpretations or quantify competing perspectives, but highlight the range of reactions and opinions that viewers might take away from a film; further research could explore these reactions in more depth, trying to connect them with larger contexts or cultural identities, and posit what such responses might mean about our broader understanding of the film.

This brief tour of different ways that *Adaptation.* might be studied and understood is not meant to be a comprehensive account of the film and its potential analyses. Rather, it suggests that no single theory is sufficient to grapple with the complexity of any given film, and how many different approaches can point us toward competing understandings of a film without clearly giving us a conclusive understanding of which is correct. Films are complex cultural objects—and some, like *Adaptation.*, are particularly complex in their structure and design—and thus we must be modest in our assertions about trying to make full sense of the text. However, diving into a theoretical approach and applying it to a single film can be a highly rewarding way to gain insights about a text, deepen our understanding of that film's connections to other cultural forms and practices, and provide greater appreciation of both a film and its cultural impact. Narrative theory offers a particularly compelling set of concepts and approaches to explore films, either on its own or in conjunction with other theoretical traditions. In the unusual case of *Adaptation.*, narrative theory becomes an essential tool to make sense of its reflexive storytelling, and hopefully the film provides a window into the compelling insights that this theoretical school offers to help become more discerning film viewers.

Notes

1 The character of Matthew is based on the real person from Orlean's book, Vinson, as earlier drafts of the scripts retained his real name. It is unclear whether the name was changed because the real Vinson refused permission to use his name, or the filmmakers wanted to overtly fictionalize him. Vinson does speak the line about not talking to her as "the Indian way" in *The Orchid Thief* (218), but there are no references to him seeing her "sadness."

2 See Charlie Kaufman and Donald Kaufman, Adaptation.: *The Shooting Script* (New York: Newmarket Press, 2002), for the published script, which was probably edited to match the final released edit of the film, rather than the actual script used to shoot the film; the downloadable earlier drafts are available on the fan site, *Being Charlie Kaufman*, http://www.beingcharliekaufman.com/index.php/scripts-writing/scripts-writing/film-scripts.

3 See http://www.imdb.com/title/tt0268126/board/thread/208700702 for this discussion thread.

FURTHER READING

H. Porter Abbott, *The Cambridge Introduction to Narrative* (Cambridge, UK: Cambridge University Press, 2002).

Narrative theory emerged out of literary studies, and there are dozens of important works of literary narrative theory. Abbott's book offers a good introduction to these approaches and key terms, covering narrative literature and the development of narratology in the 1970s and 1980s.

David Bordwell, *Narration in the Fiction Film* (Madison: University of Wisconsin Press, 1985).

A landmark book in the study of film narrative, especially in outlining a historical poetics approach, as well as in introducing cognitive concepts to understand narrative comprehension. While some of the ideas and examples are a bit dated, it is still the single most important book to apply narrative theory to film.

David Bordwell, *The Way Hollywood Tells It: Story and Style in Modern Movies* (Berkeley: University of California Press, 2006).

Extending and updating Bordwell's earlier work on film narrative, this book explores contemporary Hollywood film storytelling and style. Bordwell offers a particular focus on complex narratives, such as puzzle films and "forking path" stories, suggesting how innovative films that seem to break the rules actually adhere to many classical norms of storytelling.

John Caughie, ed., *Theories of Authorship: A Reader* (London: Routledge, 1981).

A useful collection of early writings pertaining to film authorship, including key sources from cultural theory (such as essays by Roland Barthes and Michel Foucault) and vital writings establishing the auteur theory. While numerous more recent works extend concepts and theories of authorship, this reader provides the foundation that much of film scholarship is built upon.

Seymour Chatman, *Coming to Terms: The Rhetoric of Narrative in Fiction and Film* (Ithaca, NY: Cornell University Press, 1990).

Chatman was one of the most important literary narrative theorists of the 1970s and 1980s, and this book offers the most direct application of his ideas to film. This work has particular importance for studies of authorship, narrators, and literary adaptations.

David Herman, ed., *The Cambridge Companion to Narrative* (Cambridge: Cambridge University Press, 2007).

This collection of essays introduces key concepts within narrative theory for a novice audience. While most of the essays use literature as their base, the book does cover a range of media to consider how these concepts might be translated to apply to film and other formats.

Thomas M. Leitch, *Film Adaptation and Its Discontents: From* Gone with the Wind *to* The Passion of the Christ (Baltimore, MD: Johns Hopkins University Press, 2007).

Although adaptation theory is a less developed area than other concepts within narrative theory, Leitch's work is the exception, offering a thoughtful and engaged discussion of adaptation practices and concepts.

Robert McKee, *Story: Substance, Structure, Style and the Principles of Screenwriting* (New York: ReganBooks, 1997).

There are dozens of screenwriting manuals, but there is a reason why McKee was the figure that the creators of *Adaptation.* wrote into their film—his seminars and this book are certainly the most influential sources of practical film theory operating in Hollywood over the past thirty years. Additionally, unlike most screenwriting manuals, *Story* is actually an engaging and thoughtful read, with a distinct voice and compelling ideas, even if many might be debatable as film analysis.

Murray Smith, *Engaging Characters: Fiction, Emotion, and the Cinema* (New York: Oxford University Press, 1995).

The most thorough account of characters as an aspect of film storytelling, Smith provides a crucial link between the figures that appear on-screen and how viewers engage with them. Although based on a cognitive approach to narrative comprehension, it offers a more wide-ranging approach than many cognitive film theories.

Kristin Thompson, *Storytelling in the New Hollywood:* Understanding Classical Narrative Technique (Cambridge, MA: Harvard University Press, 1999).

Thompson's approach is unusual within film studies, as it directly engages with practical theories of storytelling and screenwriting, while analyzing films to uncover their underlying structure. Her most notable claim is that films operate more on a four-act rather than a three-act structure; whether you agree with this distinction or not, her analyses of many Hollywood films offer compelling insights into narrative structures and techniques.

Robyn R. Warhol, *Having a Good Cry: Effeminate Feelings and Pop-Culture Forms* (Columbus: Ohio State University Press, 2003).

Exploring narratives across a range of media, from Victorian novels to Hollywood film to television soap operas, Warhol exemplifies feminist narratology as an approach, merging analysis of narrative structure with an account of gendered emotional response.

INDEX